HAMPSHIRE
AND
ISLE OF WIGHT
FOLK TALES

HAMPSHIRE
AND
ISLE OF WIGHT
FOLK TALES

MICHAEL O'LEARY

First published 2011

The History Press
The Mill, Brimscombe Port
Stroud, Gloucestershire, GL5 2QG
www.thehistorypress.co.uk

British Library Cataloguing in Publication Data.
A catalogue record for this book is available from the British Library.

ISBN 978 0 7524 6123 6

Typesetting and origination by The History Press
Printed and bound in Great Britain by TJ Books Limited, Padstow, Cornwall

CONTENTS

Acknowledgements

Thanks are due to Roy, for sharing stories and conversation over many years; to Cathy, who put up with me for a very long time, during which we did a lot of exploring of Hampshire and the Island in the old camper van, accompanied by our children; to Debbie, for encouraging me to become a professional story-teller all that time ago; to Nadia, for assisting me with my search for the dragon; to Hallam Mills for being so helpful, and sharing information about the dragon; to John for all the patient computer assistance; to cousin David for the photo; and to Christine Reeves of the Blackwater Countryside Partnership, for suggesting information about north-east Hampshire.

I'd also like to thank all of the people with whom I've swapped bits and pieces of story. They might be friends and workmates, or they might be passers-by who I met whilst leaning on a bar, raconteuring in a mess-hut, chatting in staff rooms, wandering down lanes and footpaths, pedalling through the forest, or sitting outside burger vans in lay-bys!

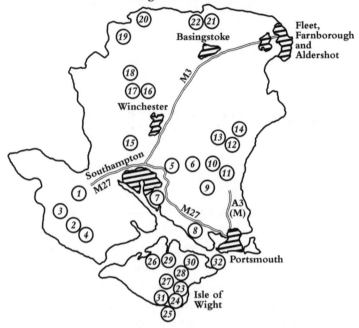

O'Leary's rough map of Hampshire, 2011
Showing locations of folk tales.

KEY TO MAP

INTRODUCTION

One winter's evening in the 1980s, I wandered across Northam Road – a main road leading out of Southampton – for a pint in the Prince of Wales. It was a wet, dark, miserable evening and the orange, sodium street lights glowed dully as the drizzle drifted inland from Southampton Water and the Solent beyond.

I leaned on the bar next to Reg Gulley and he told me the following story, which he claimed was true…

On a night like this, a young girl was seen trying to hitch a lift on Northam Bridge. A couple – who wouldn't want to be called elderly, but who were certainly of mature years – saw her from their car. They didn't really hold with picking up hitch-hikers, but she looked so young and wet and miserable – and if they didn't pick her up, who might?

So they stopped.

Sitting shivering in the back seat of the car, the girl told the couple that she'd been on a shopping trip to town and she'd lost her purse, so she didn't have the bus fare home. Home was in Thornhill, an area of Southampton not far from the couple's house.

'Oh well, we'll take you home, dear,' they told her.

They stopped just down the road from her house, and offered to walk her to the door.

'No, it's fine,' she said, 'Thank you for the lift.'

The couple drove home, but, when they got there, they found the girl's coat on the back seat of the car, all wet with the rain. Since they knew where she lived, they decided to return the coat the next morning. When they knocked on the door, a middle-aged man answered.

'We've got your daughter's coat. She left it in our car when we gave her a lift home.'

'Are you sick?' shouted the man. His wife appeared behind him.

'People like you should be put away!' she screamed at them.

Finally, the unfortunate couple managed to persuade the girl's parents that they were serious – and then they were told a story: a year ago, the girl had lost her purse whilst on a shopping trip to town, so she had decided to hitchhike home. On Northam Bridge, she had been hit by a car and was killed.

Her parents took the incredulous couple to St Mary Extra Cemetery to show them their daughter's grave – and what should they see when they walked towards the grave? There, draped over the headstone, was her coat.

That was the first time I had heard that story. Later, I came to realise that it was a generic urban legend, set in different locations all over the world. Indeed, in 1981, before I'd heard the story, an American academic, Jan Harold Brunvand, wrote a book called *The Vanishing Hitchhiker: American Urban Legends and Their Meanings*. But to me, the legend was always located at Northam Bridge – well, Reg Gulley told it to me, and he heard it from so and so, who heard it from so and so – and so it must be true, mustn't it?

But the location was so appropriate – I later heard that Wendy Boase, in her book *The Folklore of Hampshire and the Isle of Wight*, had already come across a version of the story, set on Northam Bridge, and whenever I heard versions of the story in Southampton, it was always set on, or by, Northam Bridge.

Northam, the inner city area of Southampton, where I live, is hardly the most prepossessing place in Hampshire, and Northam Road isn't at all remarkable. Yet some places have a feeling to them. The bridge crosses the river to Bitterne Manor, which was once a Roman settlement called Clavsentvm, and there are stories of lines of Roman soldiers crossing the road here, and ghostly figures guarding the way through old Clavsentvm.

It's easy to imagine, before there ever was a bridge, a mysterious traveller waiting for the ferry, and that traveller disappearing, and the boatman finding himself alone with the sound of the river and the birds flying inland from the sea. And sometimes I think I hear the sound of paddles – as if the first Belgae invaders are paddling up the lazy river, between the wooded hills. It's a very singular place – and legends attach themselves to singular places.

Invariably, the stories I hear are not told by people who call themselves storytellers, or researchers, or folklorists. The stories do not always look back to some bucolic past – often they have changed and adapted. I might hear a story from the bloke with the hi-viz jacket, who I meet at the burger van next to the exit road to Odiham – a story about a haunted stretch of road; I might hear a story from that beautifully noisy woman at the farmers' market – a story of an isolated copse which no one wants to enter; I might hear a story from a teaching assistant in a school – a story she insists belongs only to the locality she loves. Hampshire never had a William Bottrell, the folklorist who systematically collected stories in Cornwall. This is a blessing and a curse – so many stories must have been lost, but stories haven't become quaint collectors' items either; they have been free to evolve.

I work as a professional storyteller – and the privilege of this is that as soon as people find out, they tell me stories; indeed, I hardly dare mention my strange job to taxi drivers! These stories therefore amass within my poor benighted brain, and sometimes it's hard to remember who my original source was. I became a professional storyteller in 1995 – but that, of course, wasn't when I first started absorbing stories. As a greenkeeper near the Meon Valley I heard stories, as a council gardener in Southampton I heard stories, as a primary school teacher I heard stories. Often these tales attached themselves to a place; Hampshire comes alive to me through this buzz of stories and because of those special, 'singular' places – some of them beautiful, some most definitely not.

Reading stories is a strange thing. I am a story*teller*, and so am used to hearing those words, rather than seeing them in print. The concept of silent reading is, historically, a recent one; for instance, the King James Bible was written to be read aloud, which makes it so different from modern translations. In some cases in this book, I have attempted to write a story as it is spoken – though this is difficult, because spoken stories change according to the mood of the listeners, the mood of the storyteller, the state of the weather, and the place where the story is being told! Other tales are written more discursively.

If I have an aim, other than enjoying myself and hoping that others can do so too, it is to encourage the reader to get out there and explore Hampshire and the Isle of Wight. To make this easier, the chapters are ordered geographically; we start in the New Forest and then head eastwards to Portsmouth, up to the Meon Valley and west to Romsey, then along the Test Valley up to the far north of Hampshire – a sort of letter S. Then it's down to the Isle of Wight, underlining our letter S!

I do think that the best way to find stories is to get out there – to put on the boots and explore; to meet and talk to people; to listen, not just to whole stories, but to all those fragments that people mention in passing. Those stories are not just to be found in the conventionally picturesque areas either – they are also to be found in the cities, and in that strange semi-rural, semi-urban hinterland of which Hampshire has more than its fair share.

Here then, are some of those stories.

One

YTENE: THE FOREST

The first thing to say about the New Forest is that it is old; indeed it is ancient. The oak and beech woodland is typical of how much of England's landscape would have been in pre-medieval times – 'climax woodland', the mature stage of natural forest succession. However, an ancient meaning of the word 'forest' is open hunting ground, not just woodland, and this very much applies to the New Forest because it contains great stretches of heathland and bogland – some of which, like Cranes Moor, are the same today as they would have been after the last glaciation. This is highly unusual in the intensely managed landscape of England.

Much of the Forest (as the New Forest is simply known in the county) looks quite unlike the rest of Hampshire. In the 1940s, Brian Vesey-Fitzgerald wrote of 'the magnificent view over Vales Moor and Crow Hill, a view that one would expect to find in Yorkshire or Devonshire but not in Hampshire', and this holds true today.

Now that landscape has become a saleable commodity, it would cost an absolute fortune to buy as much as a shed in the

Forest, but the thing that has made the Forest such a place for stories is its marginality, its thin soil and lack of agricultural fertility; its wildness. These are the qualities that made it a refuge and lurking place for people on the margins: outcasts, dissenters, gypsies, vagabonds – those without great means and money.

Then there are the people who seem to have been in the Forest forever – the people who may have resented the Saxons and Danes as much as they resented the Normans. And it was with the Normans that the name 'New Forest' arrived. The old name for the Forest was 'Ytene', and it only took on the rather banal name 'New Forest' because it was William the Conqueror's new forest, where, as William of Gloucester put it: 'Gane of hondes he loved y nou, and of wilde beste. And his forest and hys wodes, and most ye nywe forest.'

William made the Forest Crown property, and imposed forest law. Forest law operated outside common law and protected the 'vert' (the vegetation of the Forest) and the game there: the boar, the hare, the coney, the pheasant, the partridge, the wolf, the fox, the marten, the roe deer – but, most of all, the red deer. It was due to this royal ownership that the Forest survived.

Stories have developed through the years, suggesting that William cleared the Forest of its inhabitants, destroyed villages and churches, and drove the people from their land – but there is no archaeological evidence to support this. The lack of agricultural fertility indicates that there wouldn't have been a large farming population anyway. But still, the laws were harsh; and hungry people banned from hunting deer – what resentment must that have stirred up? And how would stories from different times within the Forest have merged, and affected each other? Well, this brings us to the Rufus.

THE BLOOD-RED KING OF CANTERTON GLEN

William the Conqueror, when he lay dying, bequeathed his crown to his second living son, William Rufus – William the Red. Stories present him as a villainous ruler – this may be true, or may be partly due to propaganda, but, as no ruler at this time was much of a charmer, he was perhaps no worse than the others. Either way, it was in the Forest that William Rufus met his end, and a tangle of stories connect with this.

Sound is different in the New Forest woodland; it echoes. The bowmen would have known how to wait quietly amidst the trees. Then the peace would have been shattered as a stag bounded towards them, driven before a hullabaloo of shouts, whoops and galloping horses. One day, the stocky figure of William Rufus – easily recognised because of his red hair and beard, his even redder face, and those strange different-coloured eyes – stepped into the light and fired an arrow, which glanced off the stag as it leaped away. The Rufus shaded his eyes and watched it disappear into the dapple of greens and browns and shadows. Then another deer broke cover and Sir Walter Tyrell loosed off an arrow. It lodged in the king's breast; he snatched at it with his hand, but it broke off and he fell dead. They left him there. No carrying the body home amidst great mourning; no lying in state.

Tyrell fled to Normandy – or maybe he was just bringing the tidings to Normandy. He stopped to wash his hands in Ocknell Pond, and then got a blacksmith to shoe his horse backwards to confuse anyone who might be pursuing him. In stories, people being pursued often shoe their horses backwards, and some-times the Devil himself swivels his hooves the other way – but maybe Sir Walter wasn't being pursued.

It was William de Breteuil's job to ride to Winchester to declare the rights of William Rufus' elder brother, Robert, to the throne. Robert was far away in the Holy Land, and William

de Breteuil seemed in no hurry. He wandered to Winchester in a leisurely fashion, stopping off to have a drink here, a bite to eat there, a conversation over there, and a little flirtation just behind there. The Rufus' younger brother, Henry, who was also at the hunt, galloped straight to Winchester and had himself proclaimed king before anyone could say, 'whoopsy doopsy, the last king's dead,' after which William de Breteuil ambled in with an, 'Oh dear me, I do appear to be too late. Hello Henry, a few lands and titles please.'

So, we have the story of the accident and the story of the assassination. But the Forest is a strange place – and there is another tale, a tale that lurks deep within the psyche of the Forest; and that's the story of blood sacrifice.

Every version of the Rufus story is suffused with blood. In some versions of the story, he is said to have had a dream on the night before the hunt. There are two versions of this dream: in one version he finds himself entering an ornate church, gleaming with gold and fantastic paintings. As he gazes on them, the decorations fade away and the Rufus is in a plain, bare church – with the body of a man lying on the altar. The Rufus falls on this body, tearing at it with his teeth, desperate to swallow the flesh of the corpse. The corpse awakens, becomes Christ, and wrestles the Rufus, tearing his body open so that rivers of blood pour out and upwards, through the windows and door of the church, up into the sky, till they blot out the sun and the earth is plunged into darkness. In another version of the dream, devils come from hell to bleed the Rufus, like leeches. They tear open an artery and again rivers of blood spurt from his body and obliterate the sun. In many versions of the tale, the fleeing Sir Walter Tyrell washes his hands in Ocknell Pond, and on every anniversary of the killing, Ocknell Pond is said to turn as red as blood.

And there's more blood!

The body of the Rufus lay in the Forest until Purkis the charcoal burner came along with his cart. (Purkis is still a Forest name; until recently, there was a quality butcher's in Brockenhurst called Purkis. Sadly, it is now a convenience store.) Purkis hauled the body of the king onto his cart and transported it all the way to Winchester, along a route which became known as King's Lane. A relic of this route, near Winchester, is said to be King's Lane at Chilcomb, under

Magdalen Hill Down. The body was said to have dripped blood all along the way, so that King's Lane was a river of blood.

So another theory has arisen to explain the death of the Rufus; the theory that the killing was a ritual sacrifice. The killing took place on Lammas eve, Lammas being the festival of 'the feast of the first fruits', when bread was baked from the first harvest. The pre-Christian ancestor of Lammas was Lughnasadh, a festival where a 'king' was supposedly killed so that his blood would enrich the land. This theory suggests that the Rufus was part of a Mithraic cult, and was offering himself for sacrifice.

Historians debate the reasons for the death of the Rufus, and the debate is usually between the possibilities of a hunting acci-dent or an assassination. The ritual sacrifice theory tends not to be taken seriously, and indeed I would think it highly unlikely that a gangster (and isn't that what the forerunners of our royalty were: feuding, power-hungry families bearing all the character-istics of the Mafia?), a man interested in holding and maintaining power, would ever be likely to give his life for some abstraction. However, I'm a storyteller, as well as a frequent wanderer of the Forest, and this tale has never struck me as being simply about one historical incident. Stories can be subsumed by stories, and, in some seemingly historical accounts, there lie the shadows of more ancient legends.

Traditionally, the death of the Rufus was said to have taken place in Canterton Glen, in the north of the Forest. This is where there is a monument, called the Rufus Stone, erected in the eighteenth century to mark the site of his death. Historians, however, tend to believe that the Rufus was more likely to have died near Beaulieu or Brockenhurst, places in the Forest miles south of Canterton Glen. But Canterton Glen is a rather enigmatic place. Nowadays the A31, extending from the M27, thunders through the valley, but it is still a place with a strange feeling to it. Cantwaratun means 'Farm of the Kentish men', and 'Kentish men' doesn't necessarily mean 'men from Kent' – it means 'the other people', 'those people', 'the strange people' – and there are parts of the Forest that don't always feel friendly. Vesey-Fitzgerald, in 1949, wrote about a time when he was a child and was lost with his sister in Oakley Inclosure, a piece of woodland on Sir Walter Tyrell's route away from the death scene:

We certainly were not frightened, but I think we were both a little uneasy, I know that I was, for I felt during the walk the hostility of the Forest – and I have had that feeling once or twice since.

I've known that feeling in Canterton Glen, but I wasn't feeling a little uneasy – I *was* frightened: I was walking in the Forest without map or compass – indulging in the direction-less walking that usually finds me 'pixie-led', wandering in a circle. I had no idea where I was, but as night fell I put my sleeping bag down amidst pine trees, and fell asleep without too much trouble. In the early hours of the morning, I was awoken by the cold – not surprising when sleeping rough, even in August; but this was different, this cold came from inside me, from in my bones, and it told me that things weren't right. When I poked my head out of the sleeping bag, it was as if I was looking through night-vision binoculars – everything seemed red and slightly glowing. I pulled my head back into the sleeping bag, like a child hiding his head under the blankets, and when I finally looked out again everything had gone back to darkness. Later in the morning, I continued walking and heard the noise of traffic from the A31. I took my life in my hands and crossed the dual carriageway, found myself at the Rufus Stone, and saw the Sir Walter Tyrell pub – only then did I realise I was in Canterton Glen.

So it is that I think there is a much older story in Canterton Glen than the death of King William Rufus. Stories are slippery things, and they are quite capable of updating themselves, or attaching themselves to historical incidents.

Contemporary descriptions of William Rufus suggest that he may not have had red hair at all; his hair may have been straw-coloured. However, monks writing after the event, with an agenda based on the dispute between Church and royalty, and knowing full well on which side their bread was buttered, would easily have fitted their story into the oral narrative of the Forest. These stories of the Forest stretch back in time – to when there was still blood in the soil, and where something ancient and terrible was lurking, should you be unlucky enough to feel it.

THE WHITE STAG

Some of the Forest stags reach quite a size; it has been suggested that they can be larger than those of the Scottish Highlands. The stag is an iconic emblem of the Forest – but the greatest emblem is that of the white stag. The white stag, or white hart as it is known in pub names throughout the country, has long been a symbol of the otherworld, and the sight of it is said to portend that some important person is about to enter the otherworld. Whilst I don't wish death on anyone, I'd love to be able to say that I've seen the white stag – but I haven't. A number of times, wandering down the upper part of the Rhinefield Drive in the moonlight, I've almost convinced myself that he's standing in front of me – but I fear I was moonstruck, and not entirely unaffected by a few pints recently downed in the Royal Oak in Fritham.

The white stag appears in many stories, and the shape-shifting of a human into a deer, and vice versa, is a common

motif in stories worldwide; however, in this story the deer shape-shifts into a wild boar, which was once one of the more fearsome inhabitants of the Forest, and a much more formidable quarry for a hunter than a deer.

In the village of Burley, deep in the Forest, there lived a verderer called Robert. Verderers were administrators of the forest law set in place by William the Conqueror, so Robert had some power. Also in Burley lived Robert's sweetheart, Mathilde. The love between them had the approval of Mathilde's father, for Robert was an important young man, but it was still necessary to be discreet, so the couple would meet in the evenings in a forest glade outside the village. This glade was known as a 'lawn' – and how suburban that sounds now – but actually 'lawn' is an old Forest word for a grassy clearing in the trees.

They used to walk there separately, and, separately, they'd pass a hovel in which lived an old woman. She would always be at the doorway stirring her cauldron, and both Robert and Mathilde would avoid her gaze because her expression was so malevolent, so full of contempt and hatred, that they'd rather not have to recognise its existence.

The night before their wedding, Robert and Mathilde separately passed the old woman on their way to their tryst. As Robert approached the old woman's hovel, he saw something incredible. There, fondly nuzzling the old woman, was a huge stag, a white stag. She spoke to it, using strange, guttural words, and it responded, breathing on her, and scratching its antlers on the wall of her hovel.

'Leave the beast alone,' shouted Robert, on seeing such an abomination, 'it is the king's property.'

The insult to him wasn't just the fact that a commoner was communing with one of the king's fine beasts, but that it was such a vile and lowly commoner. The old woman turned and glared at him, and there was an ancient depth of hatred in her eyes. The stag turned and bounded off into the forest. Robert walked on, and was soon met by Mathilde. In that glade they talked about their future, and the love they felt for each other. Robert held Mathilde in his arms and they forgot about the old woman, and the superstition that it was bad luck to meet on the eve of a wedding, and that feeling of hostility that sometimes exuded from the Forest.

Mathilde was the first of the two to walk back to the village. As she approached the hovel, the old woman was standing in the middle of the lane, glaring straight at her. That stare, in all its hostility and hatred, burnt itself into Mathilde's brain, and she had to run round the old woman, and all the way back to the triangular green that marks Burley. That terrible glare haunted her dreams all that night.

As Robert approached the hovel, he noticed that the door was shut and there was no sign of the old woman. He couldn't admit to himself that he felt relief, but he felt that he was passing that hovel for the last time after one of his trysts with Mathilde, and it was so good that the old woman wasn't there. But then he saw, staring at him from an alder stump, the biggest black cat imaginable – and if the old woman's stare was malevolent, the cat's stare was positively malignant. Robert stared back at the cat, and then SCHPLATT, it gobbed the most disgusting flob of mucus straight into Robert's face. He screamed and clawed the vile stuff from his eyes, but his eyes still burned. The cat leaped from the alder stump and was gone before he could reach for a stone to hurl at it. At home, he washed his face as many times as water could be fetched for washing it – and then it was the morning of the wedding.

The wedding passed by successfully; the priest did his work, the musicians were playing, and all were dancing on the green. But then there was a shout – and the wedding party all looked at the edge of the forest trees, and there, watching them, the sun behind it, was an enormous white stag. It is hard to gaze into the sun, and the stag seemed to shimmer and change – perhaps it never had been a stag – instead it was a huge wild boar, foaming at the mouth, and charging towards them.

With shouts and screams the wedding party scattered, but the boar focused on the bride and pursued the screaming young woman round the green. It was Robert who threw his coat over the boar's massive head and leaped onto it, clinging to its neck. It screeched, a terrible noise in between a squeal and a roar, tossed the verderer over its head, and gored him to death with its tusks. It was a white stag, rather than a boar, that bounded off into the woodland.

A vengeful wedding party marched to the old woman's hovel, but she was already dead. On the face of the corpse was a smile – the first time that any of the appalled wedding party had ever seen an expression other than that of hatred on the face of the old woman of Burley.

The Bisterne Dragon

Wild boars may not be the only creatures to charge out of the woods, with the sun behind them. It has been known to happen with dragons. There were once dragons lurking all down the south coast of England – the Saxon Shore. In Sussex they used to call them knuckers, and they lived in bottomless ponds. The Bisterne dragon, however, being a more honest and straightforward Hampshire sort of a dragon, preferred the airy heights of Burley Beacon. From there, it was possible to swoop down onto the farms and water meadows of the Avon Valley, which runs down the western edge of the Forest.

A bully often likes to focus on a particular victim, and the Bisterne dragon focused on Lower Bisterne Farm. At first, the residents were able to appease it by leaving out a bucket of milk each day – but paying protection money never works in the long term, and the dragon got greedier. It already had a taste for flesh, and why hunt the Forest when cattle was there in the green fields of the Avon Valley, just for the taking? Soon the dragon had caused uproar from Crow to Winkton, and Lower Bisterne Farm was nearly broken.

It was then that the landowners and farmers knew they had to hire a lone hero to battle the beast, and so it was that they hired Sir Maurice de Berkeley.

Sir Maurice covered his armour with bird lime – bird lime is very sticky and is usually made from holly bark – and this is very relevant to the New Forest. In the Forest, there is an abundance of holly and 'of all the trees that are in the wood the holly bears the crown'. It is at midsummer that the holly king overpowers the oak king, and at midwinter that the oak king overpowers the holly king; moreover, holly is associated with the element of fire – most suitable when doing battle with a dragon. And yet Sir Maurice was a lone hero – a dragon fighter – and he'd come all the way from Gloucestershire, so I reckon his bird lime was made from the bark of the wayfaring tree.

Sir Maurice sprinkled the bird lime with broken glass, and, with his two mighty dogs running before him, he set forth to do battle with the dragon. These two dogs were capable of bringing down the mightiest of beasts, but the dragon contemptuously tore them apart and spat out the sundered canine corpses as being quite unfit for dragon consumption.

Then Sir Maurice was alone, facing the terrible Bisterne dragon, and, whilst the landowners, farmers, and peasants of Hampshire skulked in their homes and barns, the terrible battle commenced. All day the battle continued – the foul, evil-smelling beast wrapping its coils around the knight, and screeching with pain as the broken glass tore at its scales. Finally, Sir Maurice was able to sever the head of the beast, and, as the green blood burnt into the soil, he staggered from the field of battle, a broken man. He died soon after; the injuries that had so badly damaged his body seemed unable to heal. What was worse, though, was the trauma of battle – for this had eaten deep into his soul, and the mark of the dragon could never be washed away.

Now, if you travel down the B3347, you will, at Bisterne, come across a Dragon Lane, and it's very tempting to link that with the story. But Dragon Lane is probably named after the now sadly defunct George & Dragon Inn – though maybe the pub name had a connection with the local legend, who knows?

Hallam Mills lives in Bisterne Manor House, and the legend is part of his family tradition – which gives him the sort of connection and feeling for the story that I always find so important. He tells me that the battle took place in Dragon Field at Lower Bisterne Farm (now private land), and to me this has to be the place. On the wall of Bisterne Manor House (which is a private house), there is a stone carving of a dragon between fiery beacons; there is also a coat of arms with a dragon crest, and in the centre is the Berkeley Arms. Looking protectively out over the entrances of the house are two stone dogs – great mastiff-type dogs – and these are always said to commemorate the two dogs killed by the Bisterne dragon.

The fiery dragon is very much part of English folklore. There are all sorts of esoteric hypotheses connecting dragons with dragon lines across the countryside, and cosmic energy and mystical vibrations and the like. I do like a hypothesis put forward by Hallam Mills though – and it's a hypothesis that brings us back to the wild boar.

Wild boars – great beasts beloved of the Norse gods Freya and Freyja; great beasts called razorbacks by the Americans. Imagine a rabid wild boar thundering out of the edge of the Forest, a dazzling sun low over the trees. Imagine the jaws of the boar flecked with foam. Imagine two dogs, if not killed by the boar, slinking away defeated, soon to be rabid themselves. Imagine the milking stool upset and clattering – a bucket of milk would be of no avail now against a manic, enraged beast, tormented by rabid hydrophobia. Imagine screams and clamour and terrible danger. Imagine a brave knight bringing down the terrible beast – but not before the rabies virus had already begun to work on his central nervous system.

JUMP TO GLORY JANE

The dragon stories continue round the fringes of the Forest, particularly the south-western fringe, through all those gloriously named villages: Sway, Durns Town, Birchy Hill, Golden Hill, Ashley, Bashley, Tiptoe and Hordle. Say those names aloud and it's a poem!

It has been said that Hordle means 'Hoard Hill', and that buried somewhere beneath today's bungalows is a dragon hoard, and very probably a sleeping dragon. However, folklore doesn't necessarily refer to a mythical past, and in the area around Sway and Hordle there's a story dating from the nineteenth century that takes us up to the present.

Peterson's Tower at Sway is really quite ugly. The first time I saw it was from Tennyson Down, on the Isle of Wight, looking across to the mainland. I couldn't work out what that tall finger at the edge of the Forest was, or why I'd never come across it before.

Peterson had amassed a fortune as a judge in India, and, retiring to the New Forest in the 1870s, he thought that he would build the tallest concrete tower in the world. This tower was supposed to be a magnet for spiritual energy – Peterson was fond of esoteric spiritual ideas, a very Victorian habit that is the true ancestor of much modern 'new age' thinking. He used local labour to build the tower, supervising the work himself. During a time of hardship, Peterson was philanthropic, and one of the reasons for the tower's construction was to provide employment. My mate, Roy Barnard, recalls his uncle telling him that Peterson employed people to plant cabbages upside down, and then employed other people to dig them up and plant them the right way round! This may be a caricature of Peterson's employment plans, but it shows how rapidly folklore develops.

Some of the people employed in the building of the tower were from an obscure religious sect known as 'The New Forest Shakers'. Shakers they weren't – the name had been pur-

loined from the American sect. 'Jumpers' would have been a more appropriate name, because that's what they did; they jumped. Their charismatic leader was known as 'Jump to Glory Jane', though her name wasn't Jane at all, it was Mary Ann Girling. Jump alliterates with Jane, and so 'Jumping Jane' it was.

Mary Ann Girling came from Suffolk, and it seems that some grief drove her to her religious obsessions. She always dressed in black: a long, black Victorian dress, and a black bonnet with a feather pointing vertically upwards … and she would jump – up and down – up and down – into a state of religious ecstasy.

She collected followers in Suffolk, but this led to trouble and strife with the local population, and eventually they were driven out. They went down to the East End of London, where they collected more lost souls, and eventually they were driven out of London too. The sect ended up in Hordle, on the edge of the New Forest – the Forest that had always been a refuge for outcasts, dissenters and the lost.

Here, Mary Ann Girling's mania grew more pronounced – one time she even announced that the world would end at midnight on New Year's Eve. She and her followers waited out in a field for the end of the world, and then all had to trudge home, damply, in the early hours of the morning. After this, she began to believe that she was the reincarnation of Christ; she announced herself to be immortal, and then she died. A plaque was placed in Hordle churchyard:

Mary Girling Leader of the Hordle Shakers was buried here in 1886

And time went on.

One day, in the 1990s, a group of young men (though 'men' may not be a particularly appropriate description) came driving out of Bournemouth, intent on trouble and strife. They robbed a filling station just outside New Milton, and then careered off through a maze of lanes and country roads. When they heard the police sirens, they decided to dump the money. The ringleader stopped the car, saw that strange, tall concrete tower, ran into Hordle churchyard, and dumped the money behind a bush. He didn't notice the plaque on the wall. The police caught up with the young men, but the car, rather unusually for them, legally belonged to one of the gang, and the police had no evidence.

The next day, the ringleader went back to recover the money. Now, he really wasn't too bright, and he knew nothing about reading maps, so he cruised around till the evening – when he saw that unmistakable tower, and then Hordle churchyard. There was the bush, and behind it, still there, was the money. It was as he turned back towards his car that he saw something terrible at the churchyard gates. There was the tall, gaunt, angular figure of a woman, wearing a long, black Victorian dress and a large, black bonnet with a feather pointing vertically upwards … and she was jumping – up and down – up and down. Now, if a woman is wearing a heavy Victorian dress you can't see whether she's bending her legs at the knee or not – but you'd swear that this apparition wasn't bending its knees; it was straight and rigid, and yet jumping – up and down – up and down.

The young man panicked and fled blindly in the opposite direction, but every time he looked behind him there she was, always the same distance away … and yet she never seemed to be moving forwards, but was always jumping – up and down. The young man stumbled across a field – and there, ahead of him, tall and gaunt, was Peterson's Tower. Now, if you are being pursued by something terrible, surely the worst thing you can do is go down a blind alley – head for a dead end? But then, if you're terrified, the mind doesn't work logically.

The young man stumbled through the dark, gaping doorway of the tower and dragged himself up the spiral staircase. He came to an empty room, and crossed it to the next spiral staircase. When he looked behind him, there she was, at the doorway – jumping – up and down – up and down. Then to the next room – and again, there she was, behind him – jumping – up and down – up and down. And so, he continued up through the thirteen stages of the tower, till he got to the highest room, where an iron ladder led to the roof.

Now Peterson's Tower, predictably enough, was being used as a mobile phone mast, and there, in the top room, was all the receiving and transmitting equipment. As the young man dragged himself up the iron ladder, the shade of Jump to Glory Jane passed through the receivers and transmitters, fizzled and crackled – and jumped off into cyberspace.

Maybe the end of the story should be that the young man did his own jumping, and leaped to his death from the top of the tower – but he didn't. The police found him the next day, crouching in a foetal position, rocking backwards and forwards, laughing and crying at the same time. I heard that the young man is now in Tatchbury Mount Hospital in Calmore, just to the east of the Forest. He never recovered, and never seems to find any peace.

If you look out of the window of his room, there's a strange sight – a mobile phone mast disguised as a tree. In a forest full of beautiful trees, a mobile phone mast disguised as a tree is a jarring sight. Its 'branches' are perfectly straight and parallel, and it certainly doesn't look like a tree. It looks tall and gaunt, rigid and angular – for all the world like Jump to Glory Jane.

So, folklore lives and breathes — it doesn't die, it adapts. The Forest is full of folklore, which reaches back into a distant past, but, like a tree, it still continues to grow; and even when an old oak has fallen, new branches grow out of the trunk.

Two

SOUTHAMPTON

If we travel east from the Forest, we come to the city of Southampton. To leave the glades of the New Forest, and drive along a dull dual carriageway through the urban splurge of Totton, is not the most inspiring entry into a city.

Southampton does seem, at first, a very prosaic place – a city that builds its reputation on being a 'shopping city', with its new Ikea, its West Quay Shopping Centre, its Toys R Us. But, if you get to know it, there is another Southampton – a city with hidden places, sudden vistas, and a greater stretch of city walls than York. This is the city where King Canute had a palace. Well – maybe not.

In 1805, Sir Henry Englefield wrote a glorious book entitled *A Walk through Southampton*, and in this book he called a medieval building in Porter's Lane 'Canute's Palace', because if it wasn't it should have been. The story of Canute, like Coventry's story of Lady Godiva, is known nationally: that King Canute sat in his chair, facing the oncoming tide, as a 'rebuke to the impious flattery of his courtiers'. The tide continued and King Canute exclaimed:

Let all the inhabitants of earth know that vain and trifling is the power of kings, and that none is worthy of the name of king but He whose nod the heaven, the earth, the sea obey by laws eternal.

Did he hell!

KING CNUT

This king – let's drop the 'a' and call him by his old name of Cnut – this king who hacked off the noses and ears of his hostages, this vicious, power-hungry, ravaging oaf – do we really think he would make an example of himself to teach his courtiers a lesson in humble piety? I think not.

Now, Southampton has two main rivers, the Test and the Itchen. These two rivers join Southampton Water at their mouths and make the city centre a peninsula. I happen to live close to the banks of the Itchen, in old Northam. Englefield wrote that:

…it is more probable that the regal chair was placed on the sandy shore of the Southampton river [the Test], than in the black and oozy bed of the Itchen at Northam, where some have fixed the scene of this striking and characteristic story.

But Sir Henry is only going against the traditional location because he believes the sentimental story, and he wants a more auspicious location for it. Here's the more likely version:

The invading Cnut took Mercia and Northumbria, and, soon after, following the murder of King Eadmund, managed to grab Wessex, whose capital was at Winchester. There was a minor Saxon uprising in Wareham, some Danes were massacred,

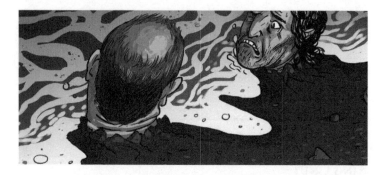

and Cnut thought that he'd wreak his revenge on the inhabitants of Southampton. Not Wareham, but it would do.

The trouble was, Southampton was known to be strange. It had the sea on three sides, and it had something quite unique: a double tide. It was said that the inhabitants had dark magical powers, powers that enabled them to control the tides. Cnut's followers, being Danes, were superstitious and feared these powers.

Cnut determined to teach his followers a lesson and, after attacking and taking Southampton, he took his captives out to the 'black and oozy bed of the Itchen at Northam' and had them buried up to their necks. The Danes then watched the tide come in and drown the unfortunate Saxons. The moral as far as Cnut was concerned was to demonstrate to his men that none of the Saxons had the power to drive back the tide. The moral as far as anyone else is concerned is that power corrupts and Vikings are vile!

The Legend of Sir Bevois

In the centre of Southampton stands the Bargate. This medieval gate used to be the entrance to the city – though now it stands strangely alone, the adjoining buildings having been demolished in the 1930s during a monumental act of civic vandalism (the sort of vandalism that over the years has damaged Southampton as much as the Luftwaffe did in the 1940s).

There are some steps that lead up to a little museum above the arch, though the museum is rarely open, being run entirely by volunteers. If you do go inside, you will see two large wooden panels, each one with a painting of a figure on it. One is of a knight called Sir Bevois, and the other of a giant called Ascupart. These two paintings used to be on the outside of the Bargate, guarding the entrance to the city, but the weather and the vicissitudes of time meant that they had to be brought inside.

At one time, all the inhabitants of Southampton would have been familiar with the stories of Sir Bevois (sometimes known as Bevis). Indeed, in 1724 Daniel Defoe wrote:

Whatever the fable of Bevis of Southampton, and the giants in the woods thereabouts may be derived from, I found the people of Southampton mighty willing to have those things pass for true.

…and those names are still in the fabric of the city; there is an area called Bevois Town, built upon a hill that was once called Bevois Mount, and at its foot is Bevois Valley. This is a fairly unprepossessing part of town now, but the names make a palimpsest, a document hidden under another document; you can use your imagination and see the hill, the valley – all rolling down to the river, before the Victorian city overwhelmed it. There is also an Ascupart Street very close to Bevois Town, and a thirteenth-century tower called Arundel Tower which is named after Bevois' mighty steed. (Rather more pleasingly, the tower is also known as Windwhistle Tower – once you get to know it, you find Southampton is full of these little touches!)

These stories are often traced back to a Middle English romance called *Bevis of Hamtoun*. Nowadays it seems that we always have to look for a written source, as if stories are only squiggly lines on paper. Yet before stories were written down they were *told*, and there is a lot of evidence of a character called Bevis before the writing of the romance. All along the south coast there are relics of someone called Bevis; he's in the landscape of the area as much as Arthur is in the landscape of England and Wales. Before the city spread over Bevois Mount, there was a long barrow on the hill known as Bevis's Tomb; on the top of Portsdown Hill (that singular hill that overlooks Portsmouth) there is another long barrow called Bevis's Grave; on the border between Hampshire and Sussex there is a long barrow called Bevis's Thumb.

Maybe there was a Saxon warrior called Bevis, who resisted the Danes or the Normans, in much the same way that Arthur is often regarded to be a Romano-Briton who resisted the Saxons. Who knows? But here is one version of the story of Bevois of Hamtun…

Once upon a time, Southampton was called Hamtun, and Hamtun had a castle – it's long gone now, except for Windwhistle Tower. In that castle there lived a boy called Bevois. He lived there with his father, Sir Guy, who was Earl of Hamtun. Sir Guy was important, but he wasn't happy. His wife had died, and so he turned his face against the world – and he showed no care for little Bevois. Often he'd lash out at the boy, and try though Bevois might to earn the approval of his father, he only ever seemed to be subject to his anger.

One day, Sir Guy was going out hunting. Hooves clattered across the courtyard as he trotted out towards Lordswood – the great forest that lay behind Hamtun and connected the Forest of Bere to the east with the New Forest to the west. Bevois ran after him and called, 'Father, Father, can I come with you?'

'Get away from me,' roared Sir Guy and kicked out at him. Poor Bevois ran back into the castle crying. Sir Guy rode deeper and deeper into the forest. 'I shouldn't have done that,' he thought, 'but ever since my wife died I've never done the right thing. Foolish it may be, but I've always blamed Bevois, since she died giving birth to him.'

As he rode deeper into the forest, Sir Guy came upon a clearing in the woods. In the clearing there was a well, and at the well there was a woman and a little girl. The woman was filling seven wooden jugs with water.

'What are you doing?' demanded Sir Guy.

'This is my job,' she said, 'I fill the jugs up with water, carry them down to the village and sell them.'

'Then I will buy one,' said Sir Guy, and lifting the jug he drank deep.

Looking at her, he said, 'You seem to be a strong woman, and a capable one. I need a wife, and a mother for the boy, will you marry me?'

'Well,' she thought, 'that's a bit sudden.' But things do happen a bit suddenly in stories – and she thought, 'Hmmmm, Sir Guy of Hamtun, a very important man – not bad.'

'Very well,' she said, 'but this is my daughter, and she's called Josyan. She would have to come with me.'

And so it was – they returned to Hamtun and got married. The wedding was wonderful; there were troubadours and harpists, clowns and jugglers, fire-eaters and play actors. They even had storytellers. (I was there myself, though unfortunately I spent the night in the dungeons for getting too drunk to remember any stories.)

Well, it would be good to finish the story there, with a 'They all lived happily ever after...' but they didn't. You see, she turned out to be not so very nice. Oh, she liked being important; she liked being the Earl of Hamtun's wife. She'd shout at the servants, 'My dinner's too hot,' or, 'My dinner's too cold,' or 'Take that servant away, give him the sack,' or 'Chop off his head!' She was terrible. As for little Bevois, she didn't like him at all. She thought that one day he'd be Earl of Hamtun, and she didn't want that. So she tried to make his life even more miserable than it already was, but miserable he was not. You see, her little daughter, Josyan, became firm friends with Bevois and they became playmates and made each other happy.

Time passed, as it does both in and out of stories, and Josyan and Bevois became older – until Josyan became a young woman and Bevois became a young man. And, inevitably, they fell in love. Now, Josyan's mother noticed this and growled to herself, 'I won't have her marrying *him*, I'll put a stop to this.' In those days, people believed that your dreams came true, so she pretended that she'd had a dream.

'Sir Guy,' she said, 'I had a dream last night. I dreamed that there was your very important-looking wooden chair,' – it was a bit like a throne, with carvings of dragons on the side – 'and Bevois crept up behind it and chopped it to splinters with an axe. What do you think the dream meant?'

The next day, she said, 'Sir Guy, last night I had a dream that you were sitting in your very important-looking wooden chair, and Bevois crept up behind you with an axe and CHOPPED OFF YOUR HEAD. What do you think the dream meant?'

Day after day she said she had these terrible dreams – though she made them all up. Finally, it was too much for Sir Guy.

'Bring Bevois to me,' he roared at the guards.

Bevois was brought to him, and Sir Guy said, 'Bevois, you must go, you must leave this place, because I think that you mean to do me harm.'

'Why, what is it that I have done?'

'My wife has had these dreams…'

'Ah – has she? Very well, I will go. I will do what they do in stories; I will go and seek my fortune.'

Bevois fetched a cloth; he fashioned it into a bag, tied it onto the end of a stick, and went down to the kitchens for some food and drink to put in it. Then he had to say farewell to Josyan. Holding each other, the tears running down their cheeks, they felt that their hearts were breaking inside them.

'One day – one day,' said Bevois, 'I will return.'

'I will always wait for you,' sobbed Josyan – because in stories that's just what you do.

Then Bevois left Hamtun – and he walked and he walked and he walked. It was a cold, grey, wet, miserable day and Bevois walked deeper and deeper into the forest. He didn't know where he was going and he knew that when he had eaten the food and drunk the drink he'd have nothing, and so, with a deep weight on his heart, he trudged on.

Night fell, and still Bevois walked – then, through the darkness, he saw a twinkling light. He followed the light through the trees and came to a rickety-rackety wooden hut. He knocked on the door, heard a scuffling and grumbling from the inside, and the door was opened by a withered old woman.

'What do you want?' She eyed him suspiciously.

'Please, good woman, could I take shelter here for the night?'

'I've got nothing, nothing to share with the likes of you.'

'I have some food and drink,' said Bevois, 'and gladly I'd share it with you.'

'Oh – very well.'

Once inside, Bevois took the bag from the stick and the old woman eyed the food hungrily. She looked so old, frail and hungry that Bevois thought, 'She needs this food more than I do,' and he gave her nearly all of the food. Indeed, he pretended that he was eating more than he really was.

When the morning came, the old woman said, 'I'm not as daft as you think, and I saw that last night you gave me nearly all the food that you had. You are a good man, and I have a present for you.' She handed Bevois a rough-looking wooden flute.

'This is a magic flute,' she said, 'and you'll know when you need it.'

'Well, it won't really do anything,' he thought, 'but it's good of her to give it to me, and it would be an abuse of hospitality not to accept,' so he said thank you, and off he went.

It was another cold, wet, miserable day, and he walked and he walked and he walked. When night fell there wasn't even a rickety-rackety wooden hut, and Bevois had to take what shelter he could beneath a gaunt tree. 'At least I have the flute,' he thought, 'and I can play a tune. I'll play a sad tune because that's how I feel.' And so he did. The tune he played, as he thought of Josyan, and he shivered with the damp and cold, and his insides groaned with hunger, would break your heart. At least, at first it would, but then his fingers started to move faster and faster – he couldn't stop them – and he found himself playing a happy tune, a fast tune, a dancing tune. Then the flute wriggled like a snake in his hands; it twisted and turned, and became a strange bell-shaped instrument, playing dancing music that echoed through the forest.

Bevois felt his feet start to move and, in spite of himself, he started to dance round and round the tree. Up in the tree there was a squirrel, and the squirrel started to dance up and down a branch on its back legs; then a badger came dancing out from between the trees on its back legs. The tree drew its roots from the ground and *it* started to dance – soon the whole world seemed to be dancing. Finally Bevois stopped playing, lay down at the foot of the tree, and fell fast asleep.

Before long, it was morning; the sun was shining and the birds were singing. 'Well,' thought Bevois, 'I'm still hungry, I still miss Josyan so much, I still don't know where I'm going – but there are things to be done, adventures to be had, and there's a whole wide world out there.' So out he went into the wide, wide world, and he walked, and he walked, and he walked … until he came to a great big house. He looked through the window and saw a very grand room. There were thick carpets on the floor, fancy furniture, pictures on the walls, and chandeliers – even though chandeliers hadn't yet been invented. Also in the room there was a flock of sheep – and a terrible mess they were making. Bevois knocked on the door; the door opened, and there stood a funny little man with a pointy nose.

'What do you want?' demanded the funny little man with a pointy nose.

'Begging your pardon,' said Bevois, 'I don't mean to be noscy, but I couldn't help noticing a flock of sheep in that very grand room. Now, I'm looking for a job. Do you need a shepherd?'

'There's no point,' moaned the funny little man with a pointy nose, 'because there's a giant, and he lives in the woods, and his name is Ascupart, and he keeps stealing the sheep. All I can do is bring the sheep into the house, and the straw and hay too – and oh dear, dear me; what a mess, what a mess!'

'Let me look after the sheep,' said Bevois, 'and I'll deal with the giant Ascupart.'

'Don't be silly; what could a little fellow like you do against a great big giant like Ascupart?'

'Just let me try.'

'Well, you can take a few of the sheep, and we'll have a trial period; but whatever you do, *don't* go to that long, narrow strip of a field at the top of the hill, the one next to the forest edge, the field called Long Acre, because that is where the giant comes.'

So Bevois looked around and thought, 'Which field has got the richest, greenest grass?' and of course, it would be, wouldn't it? It was Long Acre. The little man had given Bevois some food and drink, and so, in Long Acre, he sat down to eat and drink. The sheep were cropping the grass and bleating softly, the sun was shining, the birds were singing, and Bevois drifted off to sleep. Then, out from the forest came a HUGE giant, with huge feet, a red warty nose, a large club, and a leather apron around his belly. He leant down, picked up a sheep, and hurled it into the leather apron. Bevois awoke, leapt to his feet and shouted the Middle English equivalent of 'Oi! Put that sheep back!'

'ARE YOU GOING TO MAKE ME?' bellowed the giant in astonishment.

'If I have to.'

'Listen, I could crush you with my thumb, little man.'

'Go on, then.'

The giant roared, and leant down to crush Bevois. But what did Bevois do? He put that flute to his lips – it wriggled and squirmed and shape-shifted – and dancing music swirled around the hill top and the forest edge; and the giant started to dance. The giant was dancing, Bevois was dancing, and all the sheep were dancing around Long Acre on their back legs. The giant had the biggest, heaviest legs, so he got tired first.

'Stop, stop, please stop,' he screamed.

'Why should I stop?'

'If you stop I will go into the woods and fetch you back a special suit of armour, a special sword, and a special horse.'

'Well, make sure that you do,' said Bevois sternly.

The giant went into the woods, and when he emerged he had a rusty old suit of armour, a broken sword, and a poor old broken down donkey.

'Right,' said Bevois, and started to play again.

'No, no, no,' said the giant, 'this time I will, I will.'

When the giant returned, he brought a shining suit of armour, a shining sword, and a beautiful white horse with a black star on its forehead. The name of the sword was 'Mortglay'. The name of the horse was 'Arundel'.

Then the giant said a strange thing: 'I'm weary with being the villain, I'm weary of everyone hating me – but I have to eat. Please, could I come with you and have adventures?'

'All right,' said Bevois, 'as long as you behave yourself!'

So they took the sheep back to the funny little man with the pointy nose and set off into the wide, wide world.

They had many adventures in many lands, but one day they were walking three abreast in the wild country of Armorica. You can imagine Bevois holding the horse's bridle and the great giant Ascupart striding along beside them. Suddenly, the horse turned to Bevois and, for the first time, the horse spoke.

'Bevois, back in Hamtun there is trouble. There is a foul dragon, and the dragon is the spawn of Sir Guy's wife. A terrible dragon called Murdure flew southwards from the wild forests of Caledonia, burning and ravaging as it went. The wife of Sir Guy transformed herself into the awful dragon of the southern forest, and over Vectis [the ancient name for the Isle of Wight] they had a mighty copulation. This copulation was so terrible that it raised vast waves and storms, storms so violent that they destroyed the town of Francheville, ruined by

dragon breath and sea. The she dragon then dived into the bottomless waters of Shirley Pond, where she gave birth to a beast that grew into a mighty dragon in three days. The she dragon returned to Hamtun as the earl's wife, cool as you please. But her spawn has crawled forth from the pond and wrapped itself around the city walls of Hamtun. It is calling, "Feed me, feed me – give me my dinner." The people have brought it all the horses, the cows, the oxen, the pigs, the sheep, the goats, the cats, the dogs, the rats, the mice … and still it calls "Feed me, feed me – give me my dinner." So there has been a terrible lottery. When your number is called, you are taken outside the city walls, tied to a stake, and fed to the dragon. And the last number to have been drawn is that of Josyan, the fair Josyan. Tonight she is to be fed to the dragon.'

'Nooo!' screamed Bevois, 'but we are far away in Armorica, what can we do?'

'Jump on my back and I'll show you,' said the horse.

So Bevois jumped onto Arundel's back, and the horse leapt into the air and flew, with the great giant Ascupart running after them.

They flew over rivers, streams, fields, forests, roads, villages, towns, cities – over the sea, over Vectis – till ahead of them was Hamtun. Wrapped around the city walls was the hideous dragon. There, also, was Josyan, tied to a stake. Arundel and Bevois touched ground next to her, to see the dragon busily blowing smoke rings, and admiring them as they drifted over the city walls.

'Leave her be!' shouted Bevois, drawing the mighty sword Mortglay.

The dragon grinned a toothy grin as it lazily looked at the knight, and thought how it liked its food in tins. 'Are you going to make me?' it drawled.

'If I have to,' shouted Bevois, and struck the dragon on the nose with the sword.

'Ow!' squealed the dragon, 'that hurt!' and, seizing the sword in its jaws, it spat it up into the air. The sword flew down the south coast of England and landed in the city of Arundel (the same name as the horse, of course). To this day, if you go to Arundel Castle you will see a tower called the Bevis Tower, and in the castle you will find the sword Mortglay – all of which tells you that my story is true.

'Now I'm seriously angry,' screeched the dragon in a voice like fire and brimstone, and, blowing out a great ball of fire, it reared up above Bevois.

But Bevois drew out his flute and started to play. The music swirled around the city and over the sea.

And the dragon danced...

and Bevois danced...

and Ascupart the giant danced...

and Arundel the horse danced...

and even Josyan, tied to the stake, danced a little bit of a jig.

But as the dragon danced it shrank. It got smaller and smaller till it was just the size of a horse – and smaller and smaller till it was just the size of a person – and smaller and smaller till it was just the size of a dog – and smaller and smaller till it was just a strange green bubble. Then Arundel the horse kicked the bubble, and there was nothing left but a nasty green stain and a horrible farty smell.

Bevois cut Josyan free from the stake and they fell into each other's arms. Down from the castle came Sir Guy. 'Who are you?' he said.

'Father, don't you know me?'

'You're Bevois – and you're welcome home.'

And so it was that Bevois and Josyan were married – and later they ruled Hamtun; it is said that they ruled wisely and well (some would say that we need them back). As for Josyan's mother? Well, she went stamping off into Lordswood and she was never seen again.

Or perhaps not. There are those who say that she became a dragon again and flew, shrieking and screaming, to Burley Beacon, where she became the dragon that terrorised Bisterne. Others say that if you walk in Lordswood, you might come to a clearing, and in the clearing there is a well, and at the well you will see a woman filling seven wooden jugs with water. But if you turn round – blink – and look again, there's nothing there.

The Buried Shirt

Southampton is a modern city, and folk stories, as I've already pointed out, do not just belong to a mythical past. In 2001, the construction of a huge football stadium was completed in Northam. It was called St Mary's Stadium because Southampton Football Club originated in the St Mary's area of the city (hence the name 'Saints'). The stadium isn't in St Mary's, though St Mary's is not far away.

Now, not far down the motorway, is the city of Portsmouth – generally known as Pompey – Southampton's arch-rival. As is the way with British cities that are in close proximity, this rivalry can be deadly serious, and a local derby means that tensions run high. Normally, Saints fans are really quite civilised, and most matches pass by in good order. Except, that is, when Saints play Pompey. The police vans line up, and the air crackles with tension. Then the Pompey fans arrive. They gaze, blearily, upon the stadium – but there are some with a secret knowledge. You see, when the stadium was being built, construction workers were recruited from all over Hampshire, and this included plenty of Pompey fans. Some of these fans concocted a diabolical plot…

One stormy evening in 2001, a group of Pompey fans shuffled out to the Northam Stand end of the pitch, and began to dig a hole in what some Saints fans pretentiously call 'the hallowed turf'. Under the turf – oh wickedness – they buried a Pompey shirt. They then chanted various obscure incantations, and shuffled away, leaving the stadium jinxed.

The big opening day was 11 August 2001, and Saints marked the occasion by playing a friendly against the Spanish side, Espanyol. The terrible magic emanated from the ground and, in the first half, Espanyol whacked in four goals. In the second half, Saints woke up a bit, but they were still beaten 4-3. The jinx continued; Saints lost 2-0 to Chelsea in the first St Mary's league game, then 3-1 to Aston Villa, and 2-0 to Arsenal.

The folk story – for that's what it is – was really taken quite seriously. At one time, white witch and druid Ceridwen DragonOak Connelly attempted to lay the curse, somewhat to the derision of passing fans.

Personally, I wonder if the local Gods were upset when the blessing at the opening ceremony was made by the vicar of St Mary's Church – for St Mary's Stadium is, after all, not in St Mary's, it is in Northam – Northam, where Cnut drowned those Saxons. The jinx did seem to wear off, though, and it has to be said that if you follow the fortunes of Portsmouth Football Club, it didn't really do them much good.

Three

Dystopia – Betwixt Southampton and Portsmouth

Southampton and Portsmouth are the cities on the coast of Hampshire, but between them lies an area that has been transformed – maybe even more than the cities – during the last century.

In the 1970s, I worked as a greenkeeper just outside a village called Shedfield. At that time, it was starting to change from rural to suburban. Since then the market gardens, once so characteristic of the area, have gone. The cities have crept towards each other, and a city in all but name has formed between them along the south coast, a city made up of Hamble, Bursledon, Locks Heath, Warsash, Segensworth, Stubbington, Lee-on-the-Solent, Fareham, Gosport and Whiteley. There are stories that connect to this change – though they tend to be stories that arrive in fragments, and have to be pieced together.

Once I was reading a book of British folk tales and came

across a story about three green ladies on a hill. It was a rather fey story, and seemed related to a more powerful Greek legend about Erysichthon and Demeter. However, something about the story made me think, and I remembered a conversation I had with a policeman back in the 1980s.

At that time, the M27 was only recently built. This motorway connected Portsmouth to Southampton, then, extending onto the A31, connected to Bournemouth. This highway was to change the nature of much of the surrounding countryside. The motorway passes Hedge End, which was once a small Hampshire village (possibly at the end of a hedge) but has become a bit of an urban splurge on the edge of Southampton. The policeman told me that, every midsummer, there were accidents at a point where the motorway passes a hill at Hedge End. The drivers all related that they'd seen a naked green lady dancing around a tree, and this had taken their concentration from the road. The policeman related the story to me in a bit of a 'nudge-nudge' fashion, because the lady was naked, though the dancing could hardly be described as anything like pole-dancing.

Anyhow, in the years after this conversation, the out-of-town retail outlets and industrial estates clustered around the motorway until a time in the 1990s when, working as a professional storyteller, I was asked to tell stories on the very hill that the policeman had referred to. It was then that the fragments of story started to connect, though it was some years later that it all formed into a complete narrative. Here it is:

The Green Lady of Hedge End

Once upon a time, Hedge End was a remote village, and in Hedge End there was a farm. On the farm there lived a farmer and he had three sons – well isn't that always the way in stories? On the farm there was a hill, and on the hill there were three trees, so people called it Three Tree Hill. Every midsummer, the farmer took three bunches of primroses to the top of Three Tree Hill, and laid them out – one at the foot of each tree. This required some expertise in the finding of late-flowering primroses, given that primroses are generally all gone by midsummer, but maybe Hedge End was a special place.

As he laid the primroses at the foot of each tree, the farmer would sometimes catch a glimpse of three naked, green ladies dancing around the trees. The 'other people' can only ever be seen out of the corner of the eye, and the farmer would never presume to stare directly at a naked lady, green or otherwise, but they were there.

The farmer told his sons that, after his death, they must continue the tradition. The eldest sons promised volubly that they would, but the youngest, like Shakespeare's Cordelia, promised that he would only do what was right. This apparent lack of enthusiasm angered the father, so in his will he left the youngest son only a mere strip of land, next to the lane at the bottom of the hill. The eldest son had the biggest parcel of land, which included Three Tree Hill, and the middle son had the middle-sized piece.

The eldest sons soon forgot the tradition, which they saw as a foolish self-indulgence of their late father, but the youngest son continued taking the three bunches of primroses to the top of Three Tree Hill. This involved, of course, walking on the eldest brother's land. One midsummer the eldest brother confronted him, and demanded to know why the biggest farm was doing so poorly whilst the youngest brother's strip of a farm did so well; it had the greenest corn and the fattest pig in all of Hampshire – 'a roight proper 'ampshire 'og.' Had the youngest brother put the evil eye on the eldest brother's farm?

The younger brother told him not to be foolish – he was only doing what they had promised their father they would do. This put the eldest brother into a fury, 'a roight firk', and he told his brother that he would build the biggest barn in all of Hampshire. He claimed that he couldn't find a beam big enough to support the roof, but, were he to fell one of the three trees, he could have the beam. The youngest brother begged and pleaded with the eldest not to do it, but nothing would stop him. He took some men, horses and carts up to the top of the hill. With a felling axe, he struck the first blow. The tree gave a terrible cry, for all the world like the scream of a woman, and the men and horses turned tail and fled down the hill. The farmer continued hacking at the tree, until, with a terrible groan, it fell. Now, however expert a tree feller may be, things don't always go to plan. I once saw a council tree gang (after becoming self-employed they were no longer called a tree gang, instead they were called arboricultural tree surgeons, which I think involves a tautology) fell a tree using all the correct equipment – safety harnesses, hard hats, ropes pulling the correct way – and yet the tree spun and fell the wrong way, flattening someone's greenhouse with the most glorious scrunch. The same happened to the eldest brother; the tree spun, fell the wrong way, and flattened him.

Dear oh dear. After that, the middle son took over the biggest farm, and everyone called the hill Two Tree Hill. When six of the seven oaks in Sevenoaks were blown down by the great storm of 1987, the town didn't become known as One Oak – in the past, names must have been more fluid!

The youngest son continued the tradition, taking two bunches of primroses to the top of Two Tree Hill – and sometimes he'd fancy he caught a glimpse of two green ladies dancing sadly around the two trees. Then, one midsummer, he was accosted by his other brother, who demanded to know why his farm did so poorly whilst that of the youngest did so well. Once again, the youngest brother told him not to be foolish and drove his older brother into a ranting 'firk', so that the enraged farmer said he needed firewood, and one of those trees would supply several years' worth of firewood.

Ignoring the pleading of his brother, the middle son took the men, horses and carts up with him to the top of the hill, and he swung that 'gurt' big felling axe. The tree screamed, the men and horses fled down the hill, and the tree fell. This time it fell in the right direction, but, before it did so, a whole limb sheared off, fell, and flattened the middle brother.

The usual, rather sentimental, version of the story ends there. The youngest brother takes over the farm, is rewarded for his dutiful tradition bearing, and a lonely green lady dances around the one tree on One Tree Hill. But all is not well with the world, and sometimes all is not well for the youngest sibling; 'howl, howl, howl, howl!' Cordelia is dead. The story doesn't end there.

Unlike Cordelia, the youngest brother did survive until old age – but all would not be well for a later generation. Time passed, and down through the generations went the farm, whilst the cities grew and expanded, and Hedge End became a com-muter town on the edge of Southampton. The farm was not a rich one – indeed, it was hardly a farm. By the 1970s, it was a rough patch of land with a few horses stabled on it and an electricity sub-station. The farmer used to wear a coat with baling twine instead of a belt, though everyone reckoned he had money stashed away somewhere. He used to drink in the Barleycorn in Hedge End; I remember having a few drinks with him there one time.

Then the motorway was built and the countryside to the north and east of Hedge End was obliterated by industrial estates and out-of-town shopping outlets. Huge DIY stores, the biggest hypermarket in Hampshire, a warehouse of a shop piled high with leather sofas – shops that reduce hapless customers to blind and helpless rages, and destroy marriages.

One Tree Hill, and the land around it, was surrounded by these shopping outlets, with the motorway thundering past. Now the land was worth millions, and the money men did everything to try and get the farmer to sell. He held out for a long time, but who could resist all that money? In the end he sold – but on one condition. This was that every midsummer, a bunch of flowers should be taken to the top of One Tree Hill. You can imagine the looks of contemptuous amusement on the faces of the money men, but they agreed. In fact, why not? Wouldn't the corporate owners of the land, and all the retail stores in the area, look good – look ever so 'green' – if every midsummer the children from a local primary school went to the hill next to the superstore and put a bunch of flowers there? A photographer from the local paper would be there, and the children could be entertained by something pseudo-bucolic like Morris dancing, or, God help us, storytelling. That's what happened. And one year I did the gig, sitting under the tree telling soppy stories about green ladies, whilst a man from the paper took lovely photos. It wasn't right though, I could feel it. You see, the tree was dead; all the construction in the area had lowered the water table and the roots could no longer find any sustenance. It was the next year that my old mates, the arboricultural tree surgeons, came and felled the tree – because it was a danger to life and limb. Nothing bad happened to the tree surgeons; after all, the tree was already dead.

As for the farmer, well, he didn't quite know what to do with all the money. He bought himself a Spanish-style hacienda in the Meon Valley, and he amassed the biggest collection of country songs in the UK – all on vinyl, including several original Dolly Partons. He then decided to spend some of his money on a world tour, and this involved a 4x4 trip out into the jungle in Indonesia. That was in 1998, the year that there was a forest fire so massive that smoke drifted over Singapore. A burning tree fell on the 4x4 and killed the farmer – I read about it in the *Southern Evening Echo*. It made me feel so sad; I always thought that he was a decent man, but sometimes life just isn't fair.

Kate Hunt, the Witch of Curdridge

Of course, life never has been fair; not least for all those women accused of being witches. If we travel eastwards from Hedge End we come to Curdridge, with its singular triangle of woodland trapped between Lockhams Road, Chapel Lane and the A334. Then we come to Kitnocks Hill.

Kitnocks Hill has a strange reputation locally – or it used to when I lived in the area. When I was a greenkeeper down the road at Shedfield, my workmates told me that you could meet the ghost of a witch called Kitty Knox if you got the bus back from an evening spent drinking in Southampton, and you were 'three sheets to the wind'. It was on account of her that so many drinkers ended up in the ditch. I think I met her myself once, though my memory of events is a little hazy. I certainly ended up in the ditch.

There appear to have been two witches in Curdridge – Kitty Knox and Kate Hunt – though I think that Kitty Knox may be a generic name for any witch, and maybe Kitnocks Hill should be called Kate Hunt's Hill.

Kate Hunt was angry with the world – and probably she had good reason. The world showed little time or consideration for an old woman who lived alone. And maybe people struggling to survive, after a terrible civil war, were made to feel guilty by an angry old woman whose poverty was greater than theirs. Be that as it may, when a local landowner felled some trees and they fell across her garden – a patch of land vital for her survival – he offered no apology. The people said that Kate Hunt then cast a spell, and that is what shifted the trees from her garden to the lane; if the horses and carts were unable to get past, it was all the old witch's fault.

It was said that Kate Hunt spurned the use of broomsticks as a mode of transport, but would ride to Bishops Waltham on a farm gate. If something had happened to a gate, and the cattle had got out into the lane, why not blame old Kate Hunt, that spiteful, angry old woman? Anyway, she *would* be wicked enough to go to such a sinful metropolis as Bishops Waltham. Nowadays Bishops Waltham is ten minutes down the road from Curdridge, but I remember a conversation I had with a ninety-six-year-old man in Shedfield in 1977, and his memories from a time between the wars was that Bishops Waltham was some sort of an occasionally visited sin city. In Kate Hunt's time, maybe it was!

It was thought that witches shape-shifted into hares, and silver was the only metal that could kill a witch. So, local young men cut a silver coin in half and loaded it into a gun, and, so they said, lay in wait for the witch-hare at Pink Mead Farm (Pink is still a common local surname). They said that they shot the hare, but it managed to escape. Well, they wouldn't do anything so cowardly as shoot an old woman, would they? Later, old Kate Hunt was found dead at home, suffering from gunshot wounds.

St Peter's Church in Curdridge was built in the nineteenth century, 200 years after the lonely death of Kate Hunt, but one of the gargoyles on the church tower is said to represent her. Perhaps somewhere in England there should be a monument to all those women murdered by bullies and fools, murdered as scapegoats for the transposed emotions or inadequacies of others. Maybe, rather than a gargoyle, the monument should be that triangle of green at the top of

Kitnocks Hill – a green that may also carry a lot of happier memories: a meeting place for courting couples, a place where returning travellers were welcomed home.

At present, I believe, someone wants to build on it.

A Phantom of Combustion

There can, of course, be a certain charm in dystopia, and strange glimpses of an older Hampshire can sometimes be caught within the most alienating modern environments. If you are hurtling down the M27 from Southampton to Portsmouth, you will probably notice the River Hamble, the reed beds and the boats, but you probably won't notice Bursledon Brickworks. This is a late Victorian industrial building with a tall, red-brick chimney, where the hard graft of brick making was carried out – this area near Fareham, with its clay soil, has a history of brick making.

If you leave the motorway and seek out the brickworks, you'll discover that it is now owned by the Hampshire Buildings Preservation Trust and is being restored by enthusiastic volunteers. Should you wander round the back of the brickworks, you'll find yourself in Coal Park Lane. Here, in a semi-rural lane with a characteristic terrace of Hampshire brick cottages, you can imagine yourself in Hampshire before the Second World War. Should you wander further along the lane, you'll discover that it becomes a flyover over the motorway, leading to boatyards by the river – just a field away from the surveillance cameras and secure perimeter fence of the Air Traffic Control Centre, a startling contrast.

In the old part of the lane, there is a Victorian bridge crossing a railway line – a bridge with a sharp arch and a wall that provides a perfect leaning place for anyone wishing to watch the trains trundle underneath. Up until the 1960s, the bridge must have disappeared in a cloud of smoke every time a train passed beneath it. Sometimes, however, it is said that a cloud of smoke still envelops the bridge, late in the evening, and that a figure can be seen leaning on the parapet.

The legend goes that an old woman called Polly Crook met an untimely end here. She was a pedlar by trade, and known as a fearsome and hard-drinking old so and so; not a woman to be crossed. One evening, old Polly took up station on the bridge after spending several days drinking that distilled apple cider that the French insist on calling Calvados, as if it is only to be found in that region of Normandy. Polly called it 'good ol' foirey scrumpy' for 'twasn't it made out of best New Forest apples, and 'aven't oi walked a buggerin' lot of miles from there to yere?'. Anyhow, she settled herself on the old railway bridge, round the back of that brickworks, and got out her old clay pipe; I don't know if 'twas the spark of her old tinder box, or the sparks from a steam engine chugging under the bridge bound for old Pompey, but, bugger me, didn't the poor old soul spontaneously combust.

Three Stone Copse

If we wander westwards from Bursledon, through suburban streets, past convenience stores, over the odd patch of open land that divides settlements, we come to Titchfield. Titchfield is a pretty enough place, with a long history and a picturesque ruined abbey. It also has neighbouring market gardens that produce some of the finest strawberries in the world. Whilst the abbey is well known, Titchfield's three stones are not at all famous. One story says that they are glacial erratics; another story says something else.

Once upon a time, three noble daughters of Titchfield married the three sons of Baron Pagham. The marriages took place just before the men set sail with the mighty Sir Bevois of Hamtun, bound for Bouillon, in present-day Belgium. From there they were to join forces with other armies, bound on a crusade to Palestine.

The three daughters were left without their husbands, and spent their time doing embroidery and complaining about the servants. One night, a terrible storm hit the south coast; ships were dashed against the treacherous rocks of the Isle of Wight, trees were ripped from the ground, and the hovels of the villeins were torn at by wind and rain. Out of this fury came three young knights, who knocked on the door of the three young women and asked for shelter. The three women followed the laws of hospitality and invited them in, and the knights dried themselves in front of the great fire. They ate a fine meal, washed down with copious amounts of wine. That night, the three young women somewhat extended the laws of hospitality and took the knights to their beds.

It was that night that the three husbands lost their lives during the siege of Jerusalem.

The faithless wives were given divine punishment and turned into three stones – the three stones that gave their name to Three Stone Copse in Titchfield. (More recently they have been moved to an open wooded space at the side of West Street.) Then again, maybe the stones should be the three knights, punished for taking advantage of the three young women; or the three husbands, for gallivanting vaingloriously and destructively off to the Holy Land in the first place. Or were the three knights the shades of the three husbands? Either way, it is said that sometimes, at midnight, the three stones cross the road from one side to the other. Personally I rather wonder whether, condemned to a life of embroidery, the three young women might have thought that it was all worth it for such a night (with a knight)!

Short Road

Down the road from Titchfield is beautiful Titchfield Haven, an old harbour and a bird sanctuary. Just east of here is Hillhead. In Hillhead there is a road called Short Road. Local legend has it that it got this name because it is very short.

Tales of Sandy Lane

North of Titchfield, east of Curdridge, we have Shedfield and a sunken lane called Sandy Lane. Sunken lanes are paths that have sunk below the surrounding land, under the pressure of generations of feet and cart wheels; the flow of water running off from the fields furthers the process, as the lane provides a channel. There are many sunken lanes in Hampshire, and there are many that are more beautiful than Sandy Lane. Yet Sandy Lane is a very particular place.

When I was a greenkeeper in the 1970s, being myself part of the process that was suburbanising the countryside, our machines were stored in an old barn on the edge of a copse, just off Sandy Lane. First thing in the morning, a barn owl would glide into her nest like a huge moth. I still love Sandy Lane, though now the cottages have been taken over by bankers and computer programmers, and much of the lane is bounded by the 'green desert' of a golf course. Somehow, though, there is something about the lane that still has the feel of old Hampshire.

Sandy Lane seems to be special to a lot of people. In the 1920s, John Swinnerton Phillimore (whose descendants lived until recently in Shedfield House at the end of Sandy Lane, as did his ancestors) wrote 'The Lane'. This lovely poem carries the spirit of those old Hampshire sunken lanes:

The lane runs deep in rabbit-riddled banks.
How many hundred years of wheel and hoof
And plodding feet that good cowhide makes proof
Have grooved this rut, which lurks and winds and thanks
The burly stools of oak, the lissom ranks
Of maple and spindlewood for eaves of roof
So large they almost fend high noon aloof?
Up in the hedge the wind may play his pranks;
Here the dead-calms of the after-sunset hour
Hold every scent afloat, immobilised,
Along the leafy-margin'd air-lagoon.
Briarbush and honeysuckle and elderflower –
Each in his turn, you capture, analysed
In such retort, the essential sweets of June.

When I worked there, an old man called Jim Privett told me stories about old Sandy Lane – an area that throughout most of his life was deep country. He told me about the Apple Tree Man, who had to be wassailed every Twelfth Night – stories very much like those collected by Ruth Tongue in Somerset. I also heard that when so many men failed to return from the trenches after the First World War, the custom died out. Since then you must never pass the Apple Tree Man on Twelfth Night; he's hungry, he's neglected, he needs the respect that is his due, and he's vengeful. Jim told me this with the dead-pan face that he would assume when he told stories that he didn't take too seriously.

In the daytime, a sunken lane is a lovely place to be. At night, though, when the trees are waving in the wind, and clouds are flying across the face of the moon, it can be different – and there may be more things to avoid than the Apple Tree Man.

In a time past, but maybe not so long past, an albino badger had its sett in a copse at a bend in the lane. Strange objects were always being dug up in the fields around the lane – objects that suggested the area had been inhabited for thousands of years – and talk was that this strange beast, with the red eyes, was the soul of some ancient Briton. Doesn't the badger have that feel about it? In his poem, 'The Combe', Edward Thomas describes the badger as 'That most ancient Briton of English beasts'. In this poem, Thomas also describes how the badger was dug out, to be baited. This is exactly what happened to the albino badger of Sandy Lane.

Maybe the awe and reverence in which this beast was held was a provocation to the cruellest and shallowest of men – as the desire to desecrate a church, or wilfully destroy a work of art, can be an impulse in those who have a need to show that they can do what they like. So it was that a group of men set forth to dig that badger out for baiting.

In the copse, in the dead of night, they succeeded in digging him out; but they were unable to secure him for the dogs. Badgers are tough creatures, but this one, with its grinning teeth and red eyes, was impossible to subdue. They beat it to death with their shovels. Then a terrible dread enveloped them, like a fog, and they tried to flee the copse. It was only a copse, yet they found themselves lost, as if they were in a forest. Finally, they stumbled and tumbled out into Sandy Lane, where they heard the sound of hooves and the rattling of a cart.

'Hold you there, boys,' hissed the carter, in a voice that sounded like the scraping of bones against a stone wall, 'I'm here for you.' His eyes shone red from under a black cowl. 'Come up on my cart, my dears, we're bound for Clewer's Hill.'

One man was hauled up onto the cart, never to be seen again; another fell under the wheels; one went stark mad; and the fourth, with his hair turned white, was left to tell the tale.

I heard that on wild nights, the cart can still be heard rattling along the lane.

THE WALTHAM BLACKS

Sandy Lane leads to Waltham Chase, and Waltham Chase leads to Tyburn and the gallows; at least, it did for Henry Marshall, Richard Parvin, Edward Elliot, Robert Kingshell, Edward Pink, John Pink and James Ansell. They were the Waltham Blacks.

The resentment of the people when not allowed to hunt deer has been a motif throughout English history, as we've already seen in the New Forest. In the eighteenth century, gangs of men would blacken their faces with gunpowder and go poaching in the parks of the nobility and gentry. The following act was consequently passed; note that it specifically refers to the blacking of faces:

After the first day of June, 1723, any person appearing in any forest, chase, park, etc., or in any highroad, open heath, common or down, with offensive weapons, and having his face blacked, or otherwise disguised, or unlawfully and wilfully hunting, wounding, killing or stealing any red or fallow deer, or unlawfully robbing any warren, etc., or stealing any fish out of any river or pond, or (whether armed or disguised or not) breaking down the head or mound of any fishpond, whereby the fish may be lost or destroyed; or unlawfully and maliciously killing, maiming or wounding any cattle, or cutting down or otherwise destroying any trees planted in any avenue, or growing in any garden, orchard or plantation, for ornament, shelter or profit; or setting fire to any house, barn or outhouse, hovel, cock-mow or stack of corn, straw, hay or wood; or maliciously shooting at any person in any dwelling-house or other place; or knowingly sending any letter without any name, or signed with a fictitious name, demanding money, venison or other valuable thing, or forcibly rescuing any person being in custody for any of the offences before mentioned, or procuring any person by gift, or promise of money, or other reward, to join in any such unlawful act, or concealing or succouring such offenders when, by Order of Council, etc., required to surrender, shall suffer death.

Despite this, the aforementioned group of men went forth one night to poach deer in Waltham Chase. They found themselves being confronted by the keeper and his assistants, and it was Henry Marshall, a hard man 'distinguished by his skill in the vulgar science of bruising' (according to *The Newgate Calendar*, a lurid eighteenth-century book desciibing the lives of executed felons) who shot the keeper dead. Strangely, after the gang was apprehended, Henry Marshall lost the use of his voice – right up until the day of the hanging. They all met the drop at Tyburn.

It was after these events that the gang was given the name 'Waltham Blacks'; the news sheets of the eighteenth century could give out romantic names in just the same way our tabloids do now. There is no record of where Henry Marshall came from (maybe it was Sandy Lane), but most of the gang came from Portsmouth. Which brings us to the next chapter – let's cross the bridge to old Pompey!

Four

PORTSMOUTH

Portsmouth has been excommunicated!

In 1449 or 1450, Adam Moleyns, Bishop of Chichester, arrived in Portsmouth to do a little bit of tax collecting. A gang of sailors there were unhappy about not receiving their full wages and provisions, and they murdered him during a service in Domus Dei Church. The Pope seemed to think that this was a bad thing and put the whole town under 'The Greater Excommunication', which wasn't lifted until 1508.

One of the various theories as to why Portsmouth has the nickname Pompey is that an evangelist, who was attempting to conduct a religious revival in Portsmouth, threw his hands into the air with despair and exclaimed, 'This whole city deserves the fate of ancient Pompeii.' I may not believe this theory, but I like it.

Most of Portsmouth is on an island – Portsea Island – and there is a wonderful view of all Portsea Island from the top of Portsdown Hill. This view stretches across old Pompey to the masts of the *Victory* and the *Warrior*, a view that takes in Portchester Castle and Gosport, a view that stretches from the New Forest to Sussex, and shows a great swathe of the Isle of Wight.

I'm rude about Portsmouth because I come from Southampton, and that's what we do – but actually I can probably alienate everyone by saying that I prefer Portsmouth to Southampton. I love its vitality, its rough edges, its character – the sweep of the motorway as it enters Portsmouth over a lagoon. I love sitting in the Still & West pub in Spice Island, watching the Brittany Ferry sail out of the narrow gap between Portsmouth and Gosport, the self-deprecating, rough humour of the people in Hilsea and North End, the rough seas that race the gap between Eastney and Ferry Point as the little ferry chugs across to Hayling Island. I could go on, though I might not include Fratton Park, the Pompey FC ground. Saints supporters may point out that Fratton Park spelled backwards is 'nottarf krap' – but then I'm not a follower of the not-so-beautiful game, so I wouldn't dream of being so rude!

Spicer's Skull

The folklore of Portsmouth is as rough and ready, and full of humour, as the city, though Henry Spicer wasn't a very humorous man – he was a pirate. Mind you, in the fifteenth century most sea-farers were, when the opportunity presented itself. Spicer, though, was not at all fussy about the nationality of the ships he attacked. This was what brought him before the King's Court in 1403. Spicer made a case for himself as a representative of Portsmouth, no doubt managed to grease the right palms, and got away with it. Later, he decided to attack a French ship that was bigger than his own, the French ship sunk him, he was drowned, and that was the end of Captain Henry Spicer. Whilst some say that the area of old Portsmouth called Spice Island got its name because of the spices brought from faraway lands, others say it got its name from Henry Spicer.

Drowned he may have been, but his spirit missed old Pompey and decided to return. The spirit of Spicer haunted Domus Dei Church – a church which, since the Reformation, has been called the Garrison Church. None of the priests and prelates in Hampshire could shift him from the church – and it was only his fish-nibbled skull that seemed to do the haunting, gnashing its teeth (what teeth it had) and screaming profanities. This drove out the evensong congregation, and two members of the midnight mass congregation perished from shock.

One evening, a tailor was drinking with a group of sailors. This was not a great idea for the tailor, because his capacity for drink was nothing like that of these sons of the sea, and there was no way he could match their stories. With his head spinning, and his desperation to impress the sailors becoming more urgent, he heard himself say, 'I am afraid of nothing.'

Oh dear me – silence – then raucous laughter – then the taking of bets.

'If you ain't afraid of nothing, you ain't afraid of spending the night with old Spicer's head,' said one of them, though I'm sure he said it in fifteenth-century parlance. And there was the befuddled little tailor agreeing. Oh, sweet Jesus, Mary and Joseph help him. The very next night, he was installed in Domus Dei Church with cloth and needle and thread.

'SCRAWNY LITTLE TAILOR,' screamed the skull as it rocketed into the church, trailing seaweed and sea worms, 'GET OUT OF MY CHURCH!'

The poor tailor, gibbering with fear, bent his head to his stitching and carried on.

'GET OUT OF MY CHURCH!' screamed Spicer's skull, hovering in front of the poor tailor, covering him with putrid breath, and with rather unpleasant-looking parasitic marine worms goggling out of the eye sockets.

'I'm just doing my work,' whispered the quaking tailor.

'AM I HANDSOME? HANDSOME? HANDSOME?' screamed the skull.

'Yes Sir,' muttered the tailor, 'yes, you are Sir.'

'THEN MAKE ME A HAT.'

'I'm a tailor, Sir, not a hatter.'

'MAKE ME A HAT.'

'Yes Sir, yes Sir.'

And a fine cloth hat the tailor stitched together. Terrified as he was, and as off-putting as the noisy, hovering skull was, he was a good tailor and at heart as brave as a sailor.

'YES, YES – PUT IT ON ME, NOW, NOW, NOW.'

And the tailor pulled the hat onto the skull, and of course didn't he pull it right over the skull and tie the ends together? And didn't he take it down to the dockside, followed by an ever-increasing, lantern-carrying crowd of Pompey Polls, and screaming children, and curious sailors? And didn't he batter it against a capstan till it was all smashed to pieces, before he hurled it as far as he could out into the water?

It never returned to the Domus Dei and the little tailor won the bet fair and square.

This really should have brought good luck to the Domus Dei Church, and maybe it did, but it didn't bring good luck to Adam Moleyns, Bishop of Chichester, when he was done to death there only a few years later!

A PORTSMOUTH WELCOME

In 1714, John Carter decided to do a Dick Whittington in reverse and set out *from* London Town to seek his fortune. Being a Londoner, he must have known that the streets of London weren't paved with gold – but why on earth did he decide to go to Pompey? Neither legend nor history tells us whether he was in full possession of his marbles, but off he strode. He was still walking through the jostling streets of London, when all the bells began to toll, and the news was shouted through the streets, 'Oh yez, oh yez – the queen is dead, the queen is dead!' Queen Anne was dead.

Now, at that time, there was within the land a ferment of Jacobitism. This was the movement that, for a variety of often contradictory reasons, wanted to restore the Stuart dynasty to the throne. The Jacobites wanted James Stuart to be king, but George, Elector of Hanover, had been declared Anne's successor.

John Carter wanted a new life;
James, George, King and Crown
John is marching to Pompey town

So it was all the same to him. His pack was on a stick, the stick was over his shoulder, and his feet were on that dodgy road to Portsmouth. He braved the footpads and cutpurses of the Surrey heaths and Eashing Bridge, he risked the highwaymen of Hindhead Common and the Devil's Punch Bowl; indeed, he may have passed the tarred body of a highwayman dangling on a rope at the top of Gibbet Hill. He trudged the narrow valley between Butser Hill and War Down, between thickly forested hills inhabited by inbred robbers, until eventually he reached Portsdown Hill and a breathtaking view over the Solent. The ships were a-bobbing at anchor, he saw the long ridge of the Isle of Wight, and all of Portsea Island was beneath him.

John Carter reached the sentry at Ports Bridge and announced, as seemed only proper for one from the capital, 'Queen Anne is dead.' The news reached Sir John Gibson, the governor. Now, rumour had it that the governor had Jacobite sympathies; maybe Sir John thought that to pay attention to a dust-covered lunatic fresh into town, making dangerous announcements, would be to draw suspicion on himself, or maybe he was just applying a traditional Portsmouth welcome. Either way, he had John Carter flung into jail.

It wasn't so long afterwards that an official messenger arrived with the news, and so Carter was released. This is Pompey, though, and everyone likes a good wind-up. Throughout the rest of Sir John Gibson's governorship, officials would love to whisper – loudly – 'Pray, is Queen Anne dead?' and watch him turn apoplectic.

As for John Carter, he married Susanna Pyke and became a successful merchant, and also a Rational Dissenter who refused to belong to the Church of England. His son, also called John Carter, became nine times Mayor of Portsmouth, and also played a key role in diffusing the crisis caused in 1797 by the great naval mutiny at Spithead.

John Carter Junior was also a Rational Dissenter, and therefore a worthy and sober fellow. A lot of his money seemed to come from running a distillery and being a brewer, but then this is Pompey, and his father had been welcomed to town in a traditional Pompey manner.

Riots and the Gallows

In 1782, whilst John Carter Junior was mayor, a Scotsman called David Tyrie was convicted for sending intelligence to the French about British fleet movements out of Portsmouth. The judge ruled that he be taken to the Portsmouth gallows on Southsea Common and be hanged, taken down, disembowelled, castrated, beheaded, and then his body should be quartered. He dangled on the rope for twenty-

two minutes; one can only hope that he died during the hanging.

This is when the Pompey crowd came into its own. Spectators pushed forward so close that the blood from the disembowelling spurted over them, and that's when the fighting started. Well, everyone wanted a souvenir – a finger would be good for a pipe stopper; a handkerchief covered in treasonous blood would look good hanging on the wall. The military were called and the mob pelted them with stones. This was not a revolutionary mob, this was just a Pompey mob – out for a riot, we want bits of body.

The body was put in a coffin and buried under the shingle on the seashore. As soon as the officers retired, a gang of sailors dug the body up, hacked it into pieces and distributed the bits all around the fleet as souvenirs. Meanwhile, the head was grabbed by the keeper of the Gosport Bridewell and exhibited in a glass jar on the bar of his pub for many years, until it was stolen by another group of sailors. It may not have looked any more disgusting than many a jar of pickled eggs I've seen in various Portsmouth and Gosport pubs over the years. But this is Pompey, and typical of the place – all of which leads me to the story of Jack the Painter.

The Corking Up of Jack the Painter

Jack's story is not dissimilar to that of David Tyrie – only it seems to have generated more folklore. James Hill, alias James Hinde, alias James Aiken, nicknamed Jack the Painter, was another revolutionary Scotsman. His sympathies with the struggles of the American colonists led him, in 1776, to attempt to set fire to the rope houses in Portsmouth Dockyard. These long buildings are still there, in the Historic Dockyard that houses the *Mary Rose*, HMS *Victory* and HMS *Warrior*, and were designed so that, during manufacture, the ropes could be fully stretched out. Ropes and rigging were, of course, vital for the functioning of the British Navy.

Jack failed in his task. He was eventually apprehended and sentenced to hang from the mizzen-mast of the *Arethusa*, the mast being placed at Portsmouth Dockyard gates. Jack wasn't given the benefit of a clean drop – he was hauled up into the air, to dance and choke his life away with a fine view over Portsmouth Harbour, as a warning to others and, of course, as a spectacle for the bloodlust of the inhabitants of Pompey. The body was then flung into a boat and rowed out to Fort Blockhouse, to be tarred and hung up in chains. Fort Blockhouse commands the entrance to Portsmouth Harbour, so, as ships glided through the narrow entrance between Pompey and Gosport, all the crew would be treated to the sight of the punishment for treachery.

Then, along came another group of drunken sailors – and they climbed up the gibbet, stole the corpse, and flogged bits of the corpse to pubs all over Portsmouth and Gosport. The head ended up on the bar of the London Tavern (the site of the present-day Ship Anson Inn), just opposite the dockyard gates where Jack had met his end. But the London Tavern didn't just get the head of Jack the Painter; it also got the ghost.

Now, Jack the Painter had spent so much of his life on the run, that in death he fancied a bit of comfort. So he took to haunting the lodgings upstairs – and 'lodgings' isn't a good enough word, for this was a fine tavern with lodgings fit for naval officers. One room had a grandfather clock, a fine fireplace, and a bookcase full of nautical almanacs. On account of the bookcase, it was known as 'The Library'. The ghost loved this room: just right. Well, no one wanted to lodge in this room, what with the ghost of Jack the Painter howling at them and jeering that the bloody French had joined in the American War of Independence, so the landlord was losing money hand over fist.

'Get rid of that bloody 'orrible head!' said the landlord's wife. So he took it down to the quayside and slung it as far as he could out to sea. Glug glug glug, it sank down to the bottom and came to rest grinning at the skull of Captain Henry Spicer (which had miraculously rebuilt itself) whilst fish swam into one eye socket and out of the other one.

Well, they got rid of the head, but did they get rid of the ghost? No – it just got worse. I'll tell you what it looked like. It was very tall – 7ft tall – because all that dangling on a rope had stretched Jack. It had long, green hair like seaweed, round staring yellow eyes, and a mouth like the mouth of a blob fish – and if you don't know what a blob fish looks like, I assure you, you don't want to know. As for the ghost's feet – this may be the worst part – they dangled 2ft off the ground.

'Get the vicar in, he'll exorcise the bloody ghost!' screamed the landlord's wife. So, along came the vicar from the Garrison Church – at that time they hadn't quite finished building St Anne's Church in the docks. In went the vicar with bell, book and candle – but a few minutes later he was out again, running screaming up Commercial Road with his hair standing on end. He may only have had two strands of hair, but they were vertical!

'Get the vicar's boss in!' bellowed the landlord's wife, 'get the bishop.' So the bishop came down from Winchester, because at that time there wasn't a Bishop of Portsmouth. (The Roman Catholic Church had a cardinal in Rome with responsibility for the evangelisation of Portsmouth, but, given that he was called Hyacinthe-Sigismond, he never dared set foot there.) Next minute, though, the bishop had picked up his skirts and fled up Commercial Road.

'Get the bishop's boss – the Archbishop of Canterbubble!' screeched the good lady – but he wouldn't come anywhere near Pompey, and I shouldn't imagine that he'd have been able to shift the ghost either.

Well, they were in despair now – but then the landlord's wife remembered old Jeremiah. Now, Jeremiah had been at sea for years, and it was said that he had a way with ghosts, on account of some terrifying cult he had encountered in Java. Leastways, he was afraid of nothing.

'I'm desperate, I'll try anything,' said the landlord, and went down to the quayside where he encountered old Jeremiah, with his tarry pigtail and tarpaulin hat, sitting on a capstan and smoking his old clay pipe.

'Can you deal with ghosts?' asked the landlord.

'What's it to you then?' growled Jeremiah, who wasn't the most affable man.

'I'm the landlord of the London Tavern…'

'Aye – you have the ghost of Jack the Painter. You'll want him shifted. I can see you right if you see me right,' said Jeremiah, rubbing his thumb and forefinger together.

Well, after a lot of bargaining they came to an agreement – and Jeremiah promised he'd come to the London Tavern that night, provided he was also supplied with one bottle of beer, seven pots of beer, three noggins of gin and peppermint, eight pints of porter, a quart of rum, a loaf of bread, a pot of oysters, a pot of shrimps and an apple.

That night, Jeremiah rolled up to the London Tavern, and upstairs they went to The Library. 'Here's the key,' said the landlord, and off he went as fast as he could.

Well, old Jeremiah locked the door and pocketed the key. He sat himself down, drank the bottle of beer, ate the oysters, shrimps and bread, had a little bit more beer, drank the gin and a few drops of rum, and then had the apple and porter for pudding. After this, what with the crackling of the fire and the tick-tock-ticking of the grandfather clock, he drifted off to sleep. He woke up when the grandfather clock stuck thirteen.

When a clock strikes thirteen, you know something's wrong. If a church clock strikes thirteen, the bodies pop their heads out of their graves; if a ship's bell sounds thirteen times – indeed, any more than eight times – the ghosts of dead sailors are liable to clamber aboard. When the grandfather clock in The Library of the London Tavern struck thirteen times, everything went icy cold, and the fire flickered and went out. Jeremiah opened one bleary eye and regarded the hideous apparition hovering in front of him. It screamed and howled in a most terrible manner.

'Silence there, shipmate, or I'll have you overboard,' said Jeremiah.

The surprised apparition shrieked at him again.

'What do you want, you bloody noisy lubber?' said Jeremiah, opening the other bleary eye.

'I want ye to run away,' screeched Jack.

'Why?'

'I don't know!' howled the ghost, 'I'm a ghost, that's what I do.'

'I ain't running from no ugly ghost,' said Jeremiah, taking a swig of porter, and belching. 'Anyhow, how did you get in here? You're over a fathom tall and twice as ugly; I locked the door and I have the key in my breeches pocket. How'd ye get in?'

'I CAME THROUGH THE KEYHOLE!' screamed the ghost triumphantly, as if this was proof of its spectral credentials.

'No, ye never.'

'I DID, I DID, I DID!' screamed the ghost, bouncing all around the room, its green hair sticking out in all directions.

'I'd as soon believe ye could come through the keyhole, as believe ye could get into this bottle,' said Jeremiah slyly, holding up the beer bottle.

'Easy,' said the ghost, and, taking a deep breath, he got smaller and smaller and smaller and − POP − in with him into the bottle. Jeremiah, of course, shoved the cork back into the bottle, took a swig of rum from another bottle, and went back to sleep.

'Let me out, let me out!' called the ghost from the bottle, but Jeremiah was already snoring.

Well, in the morning, Jeremiah took the bottle down to the quayside and lobbed it into the briny. Now, some say it floated across to the Isle of Wight, and that is why Carisbrooke Castle is haunted, though how it could float upstream along the River Medina defeats me. Others say it floated way out to sea and was picked up many years later by one of the crew of the *Titanic*, but I reckon that's just one of those stories.

I know what happened to Jeremiah, though. The landlord was so grateful to him for getting rid of the terrible ghost that he gave him free drinks for the rest of his life. It is said that nowadays, should you go into the Ship Anson pub, built on the site of the old London Tavern, you might see another ghost. But it makes no noise, and causes no disturbance. It's just the ghost of old Jeremiah, sitting in the snug, having a drink and smoking his old clay pipe.

COMMANDER CRABB

The folklore of Portsmouth – probably because of Portsmouth's association with Nelson and the Napoleonic Wars, and because of the presence of HMS *Victory* – is often associated with the late eighteenth and early nineteenth centuries. However, as with Southampton, the folklore doesn't just stretch back into the past; it also lives and breathes and grows.

Given that Portsmouth is a naval city, built on an island, it is hardly surprising that the stories drip with salt water. Sometimes, at night, a trail of salt water can be seen connecting two Pompey hostelries: the Keppel's Head Hotel, near the dockyard, and the Sally Port Inn in Spice Island. Should it be the early hours of the morning, and should a sudden chill have descended, and should you suddenly be enveloped by the smell of the sea, and should you listen carefully, you might hear the flap, flap, flap of fins. You may think, after you've stopped running, that it is some sea monster looking for a nice dinner, flapping along and staring through goggly eyes. Of course, it does have fins and goggles – not because it's a sea monster, but because it's the ghost of the diver, Commander 'Buster' Crabb.

In April 1956, Crabb disappeared in Portsmouth Docks, whilst diving under the Soviet cruiser *Ordzhonikidze*. This

cruiser had brought Nikita Khrushchev and Nikolai Bulganin on a diplomatic mission to Britain. Crabb's body wasn't found till June 1957, floating off Pilsey Island in Chichester Harbour, minus its head and hands.

Commander Crabb had been recruited by MI6 to investigate the Soviet cruiser, and theories abound as to how he met his end. It could have been Eduard Koltsov, a Soviet frogman, who cut his throat during an underwater battle. He could have been shot by a Soviet sniper. Wilder conspiracy theories have arisen to say that Crabb was thwarting an attempt by white Russians to blow up the ship, or that *he* was trying to blow up the ship, or that he had defected to the USSR and that the body found at Pilsey Island wasn't his – or even that MI5 had discovered that he was about to defect and sent another frogman to kill him. Whatever the truth may be, there is such an aura of Cold War mystery over his death, that the incident has morphed into folklore, and his ghost has joined the legions that haunt old Pompey.

Both the Keppel's Head (heads seem to abound in the Portsmouth stories) and the Sally Port have claimed the ghost of Commander Crabb, and it isn't known which hotel he stayed at on the night before he disappeared because, strangely, the relevant page has been torn out of the registers of both hotels. Perhaps he stayed in one, and ate in the other. There are some lovely stories, though, suggesting that he was staying in the one, but visiting a certain lady in the other; and some of those stories suggest that there is a great camaraderie of divers throughout the world, and that the lady in question was the wife of a Russian diver on board the *Ordzhonikidze*. This is certainly entirely fictitious, but what a wonderful story it would be: Cold War intrigue, love, sex, betrayal – both political and sexual – but then aren't these the elements that make folk stories? Folk stories in books are often presented as being only about fairies and bucolic country scenes, but that's not the way folk told them to folk!

Should you talk to anyone who has meandered, in a rather disoriented condition, through the streets of old Portsmouth in the early hours of the morning (and I certainly know one), they will tell you that there is a flippered phantom that flap, flap, flaps between the Keppel's Head and the Sally Port, and they will tell you about the smell of the sea.

And imagine – down in the murky depths of Portsmouth Harbour, the place from which the *Mary Rose* was lifted, the muddy seabed littered with Tudor artefacts, bits and pieces from Napoleonic times, shards and fragments of British history. Imagine the spectres of all those dead sailors, those who went to sea and never came back, the Spithead mutineers, the men and women of Pompey, those hardened women who survived Spice Island, and those who didn't. Imagine the ghosts of a procession of dead mariners, festooned with seaweed – and imagine Commander Crabb fighting a battle with an unknown assailant, getting his throat cut beneath the looming hull of the *Ordzhonikidze*.

Five

The Meon Valley

If we travel north of Portsmouth, and just a little to the east, we come to the Meon Valley, which is named after the Meon Warra, a Jutish tribe that rowed up the river in the sixth century. Whilst the New Forest is famous nationally, the Meon Valley isn't so well known, but it really is one of the beauties of Hampshire, and is an area rich in folklore. As Hampshire wasn't a county that had an enthusiastic and dedicated Victorian folk story collector, like William Bottrell in Cornwall, these stories have to be found in fragments – and in the telling of these fragments, we see what happens with the unconscious process of story building. (It is worth noting that there were two enthusiastic folk *song* collectors active in Edwardian Hampshire: Henry Hammond and George B. Gardiner.) I heard fragments of stories in the 1970s, particularly from a bunch of venerable Hampshire squeeze box players who used to make merry in Sam's Hotel in Shedfield (now called Samuel's Rest), and these fragments suggested a rich folklore.

The River Meon rises just south of the village of East Meon, a village with a dramatic chalk escarpment rising to the sky behind a beautiful Norman church. The river flows north-east round a ridge for a while, before deciding to flow southwards from Warnford. It reaches the Solent at the lovely little harbour of Hill Head, which, with the marshes of Titchfield Haven, is an oasis in the dystopia described in Chapter Three. The seventeenth-century writer and fisherman, Izaak Walton, wrote, in *The Compleat Angler*, that the River Meon was the best river in England for trout. The Meon Valley itself fades away as the river approaches Wickham, so we'll start our tour at Wickham, and travel northwards. We'll begin with a punch-up and an old bruiser called Sixpenny Moses.

SIXPENNY MOSES AND TANGLEFOOT TOOP

Sixpenny Moses was a prize fighter, with a preference for six-penny beer – the price of a gallon of ale in the 1860s. He came from West End, a village in between Southampton and Hedge End, and would travel the villages of Hampshire looking for a rumble, with bets being cast. He would fight fist-a-cuffs with his adversary, on the side of a ditch, each attempting to knock the other into the ditch. A law had been passed which banned bare-knuckle boxing, but oft times the local 'bobby' would watch, take a bet himself, and only intervene if things got really nasty.

Now, every May there is a horse fair in Wickham, and it attracts gypsies and travellers from far afield. At that time there was a great Romany prize fighter known as Tanglefoot Toop. Toop was considered to be a bit flash, and grizzled old Sixpenny Moses arrived at Wickham Fair intent on giving the flash traveller a good thumping.

They were soon opposite each other, Sixpenny lashing out with his enormous fists at the much more slender and agile Toop. The fight entered folklore because the local country people insisted that Toop used a dark, Romany spell that entangled the legs of poor Sixpenny Moses and caused him to tumble into the ditch all unawares, and that Toop's victory was therefore most unfair. However, stolid Hampshire countrymen, nicknamed Hampshire Hogs, don't like to lose – especially to someone with a rather quick and fluid way about them – and it's possible that Tanglefoot was just too quick, and Sixpenny swung so hard at an empty space that he took a tumble into the waiting ditch. As Sixpenny floundered around in the brackish water at the bottom, Tanglefoot was heard to say, 'Let God part those waters for you, Moses,' before being carried away, shoulder high, by a crowd of cheering travellers. This didn't endear him to those sullen Hampshire Hogs.

The Wickham Horse Fair is still held every year, and the quiet and prosperous village of Wickham is transformed for a day every May – jaunting carts and horses galloping up and down the street, beer being drunk, bargaining taking place. In 2009, there was the beginning of a bare-knuckle fight at Wickham Fair – not a run-of-the-mill punch-up outside a pub, but a prearranged fight. It was soon broken up by the police.

A lot of folk tut-tutted about the travellers, and the *Daily Mail* described it as a 'barbaric scene'. I have been told, though, that you can sustain a lot more damage from being smashed in the head by a large, modern, boxing glove, than by a bare fist. If we need to disapprove, maybe we should look at the televised, big business version, rather than a prearranged grudge match at Wickham Fair. Mind you, I bet there was a fair few quid going on it!

St Wilfrid

Wilfrid came to the Meon Valley in 681 and his name has been in the Meon Valley stories ever since. There is a pilgrimage trail dedicated to St Wilfrid that connects the beautiful churches of the Meon Valley, and it's a wonderful way to explore the course of the river. A lot of the walk is along the course of the now disused Meon Valley railway, which provides a great path. Walking along the A32 is definitely not recommended; the traffic travels very fast and there is little room for the pedestrian – it is a very dangerous road for walkers.

The Venerable Bede tells us that before the arrival of St Wilfrid, the inhabitants of the Meon Valley were 'ignorant of the name and faith of God'. In this godless state they were hit by a terrible famine and often 'forty or fifty, being spent with want, would go together to some cliff, or to the sea-shore, and there, hand-in-hand, miserably perish by the fall or be swallowed by the waves'. The river was teeming with fish, but somehow the poor, ignorant heathens of the Meon Valley were only able to catch eels. Wilfrid cast his nets, immediately caught 300 fish, and the thankful Meon Warra converted to Christianity forthwith.

It is, of course, interesting how propaganda works, and the propaganda surrounding St Wilfrid seems not to baulk at this rather sacrilegious comparison to Jesus himself. Wilfrid was actually a very able, scheming, politician and power broker. He came from Northumbria and, when he was a boy, he had studied at that centre of Celtic Christianity, Lindisfarne, after which he travelled to Rome. On his travels, he had been seduced by the luxury and power of the Roman Church, and so in England he became its power broker. At the Council of Whitby in 664, it was Wilfrid who championed the cause of the Roman Church against the Celtic Church, and it was Wilfrid who won the case for Rome, and the idea that

Christianity was a set of beliefs to be imposed by authority, rather than something that lived within the people. It was during four or five years of a fascinating and turbulent life that Wilfrid visited the heathen, Saxon and Jutish south of England. He set up a church in Selsey, which was the base for his forays up the Meon.

The churches along the Meon are all beautiful, but, to my mind, one church is the loveliest, though it is by no means the finest. That is a church with no saint's name attached – it is known only as Corhampton Church. The leaflet describing the Meon Valley pilgrimage says: 'Many think that the church ought to be called St Wilfrid's because of the bishop's strong association with the site'. I can only write, 'thank God it isn't', because Corhampton Church has a feel to it which is the very antithesis of that politically astute, powerful politician, Wilfrid. The place seems genuinely holy.

The church is built upon a mound within a circular enclosure, a mound that suggests the place was holy before the arrival of Christianity. The church itself is pre-Norman conquest and very simple – simple, unfussy and spare. Outside the church is a yew tree that may be more ancient than the church itself, and inside, in 1968, some twelfth-century wall paintings were uncovered. In medieval times, the walls of a church would have been emblazoned with pictorial storytelling. The Bible was a closed book (pardon the pun) for most people: firstly, because most people couldn't read, and secondly, because it was in Latin – the language of the ruling class. Inside the church was another 'bible', sometimes known as 'The Poor Man's Bible', though undoubtedly it referred to women as well! This was a colourful array of pictures covering the walls, telling stories; they were whitewashed over during the Reformation. These stories were biblical, but were also intensely local – so the religious storytelling of the people must have been very tied up with their own myths and legends, and their own landscape. Inside Corhampton Church, the stories seem to be about a saint other than St Wilfrid, a much more appealing saint called St Swithun. This could be the cue to tell some of those stories, but they are so much associated with Winchester that I'll leave them for the next chapter. Instead, we'll take a little walk behind the church, past the Punch Bowl, across Beacon Hill Lane, through Corhampton Forest and onto Sailor's Lane. Now we'll take the Wayfarer's Walk from Sailor's Lane, and we'll find ourselves entering Betty Mundy's Bottom, which is a wooded valley heading up to Preshaw Down.

BETTY MUNDY'S BOTTOM

In a 'once upon a time' sort of a time – a time that belongs to stories; a time that carries Napoleonic elements, and elements of a more mythic age of kings and castles – there were three sailors. These three sailors had been paid off at Portsmouth, and, having spent all their money in Spice Island, were heading to London to sign on another ship. They seemed to have strayed from the Portsmouth–London road, but then that road was a grim and dangerous thoroughfare, bedevilled by robbers, rogues, cutpurses, villains, foot-pads, low-pads, high-pads, ruffians, scamps, snafflers, toby-gills, skull smashers, and murdering, thieving, highwaymen, so a diversion was often made. Thus the three sailors meandered up the side of the Meon Valley.

Night fell, and the sailors found themselves in Betty Mundy's Bottom. They decided to light a fire and sleep under a tree, with only half a bottle of rum left between them. One sailor kept watch in case there should be any robbers, rogues, cutpurses and etc.

''Allo my babes,' said a voice in the tree. The sailor looked up, and there, in the tree, was a fairy.

At this point, I must discuss the vexed subject of fairies. In a lot of the old Hampshire stories, the fairies were not little sylph-like beings with gossamer wings, but substantial beings whose efforts at flight were sometimes hampered by their not inconsiderable bulk. This fairy was called Betty Mundy, and she was a rotund, buxom, jolly, red-faced lady, with a smile so broad it seemed to go from one side of her round face to the other.

'Spare us a drop of rum, Jack,' said the fairy to the astonished sailor. She took a good swig, and then asked him what three sailors were doing in her forest.

'We're on our way to London Town,' said the sailor, 'and we've no money left, and we're starving hungry.'

'Well now, here's a present for you – a cloak to save your feet,' said Betty, and handed him a cloak before she vanished.

Fearing ridicule, and thinking he must have imagined the whole thing, the sailor made no mention of this when he woke up one of his mates to take his turn at sentry duty.

''Allo my babes,' said Betty – and don't we go through the whole thing all over again. This time, though, when the sailor complained of having no money, she handed him a purse, saying, 'Here's a present for you, my luvver, a purse to save you work.'

When he woke the third sailor without mentioning events, and the third sailor took up his post, Betty gave him a 'horn to save you fist-a-cuffs,' before she vanished.

Come the morning, the sailors found their gifts still there, so they told each other what had taken place and then emptied out the purse. Leastways, it never could be emptied; it just kept on producing gold and silver coins. Wonderful, wonderful. No need to walk to London, no need to sign on some bloody, leaky hell ship; soon they had got themselves a pub, built like a castle, and there they were: dressed like three fine gentlemen.

Now, King Stephen, who lived in the castle on Stephen's Castle Down, got to hear about the three fine gentlemen, and, given that he had a daughter of marriageable age, and he wasn't going to marry her off to some thick Hampshire Hog, he invited the three fine gentlemen to tea. What people didn't know was that the princess was also a witch, and a bitter foe of Betty Mundy. I'd put all that down to jealousy; the princess was all pale and slim with flaxen hair – so wouldn't she envy a fine, plump, lump of a woman like Betty Mundy, a woman who never thought a jealous thought?

Well, the sailors, with fine powdered periwigs on their heads (the tar having long grown out of their hair), set out in a coach and horses for Stephen's Castle. There was much foll-de-lolling and lah-de-dahing, and one of the sailors found himself walking arm-in-arm with the princess; I believe that this is known as 'dallying'.

'From whence dost thy fortune come?' quoth the princess, 'hast thou inherited it from thy forebears?'

The foolish sailor thought that he would impress her with his magical powers, and so, drawing forth the purse, he said, 'Money is no object to me – I have as much as I want.' And the eyes of the wicked princess glinted, and she thought, 'Mine – mine – mine! I want – I want – I want!' and, as soon as she could (which was quite soon), she nicked the purse and sub-stituted another one. The sailor's purse may have had magical powers, but it looked like a purse generally fashionable at the time – the time being 'once upon a time'.

Well, the next day, back at the pub, the sailor looked for a few quid to buy a paper and – no money. He shook and shook the purse, but nothing, and finally he twigged what had happened. 'Now,' said the sailor with the cloak to save your feet, 'we'll try this out,' and he donned the cloak, wished himself into the princess's bedroom, and there was the purse. Before he could grab it, though, in came the princess.

'Thief! Intruder! Burglar! Sailor in my bedroom!' she screamed, and a hurly-burly of soldiers, guards and pikemen came rushing in. The sailor panicked, and it is hard to make a wish with a veritable army descending on you, so he ran to the window and jumped. Oh dear – the cloak snagged on the window, and the sailor tumbled, cloakless, into the moat.

When the bedraggled sailor arrived back at the pub, it was time for the third sailor to use his horn to save fist-a-cuffs. The three of them walked to the foot of the castle, the sailor blew the horn, and a terrible spectral army blew in like marsh mist, hissing and sighing – from King's Copse and Sergeant's Copse, from Corhampton Forest and the Punch Bowl beneath Beacon Hill. The soldiers surrounded the castle and stamped their skeletal feet, rattled their swords and ground their teeth. The sailors called out that if their treasures weren't restored to them, they would lay siege to the castle and starve everybody out.

The princess may have been evil, but she was certainly brighter than the sailors, and she immediately saw the flaw in the plan. Putting on the cloak, she wished herself next to the sailor with the horn, grabbed it, and, before he could say, 'splice my mainbrace and blow on my horn,' she wished herself back into the castle. The army faded back into the landscape, and the sailors were left standing in a field, looking like three scarecrows.

Well, they had the pub didn't they? That soon went to wrack and ruin because they drank too much, gave too much away, and sold too little. They were, after all, still sailors at heart. Finally, with nothing left, they decided to go their separate ways. One said he'd carry on up to London Town; another said he'd take the road back to Portsmouth; and the third said he'd head for Bristol via Lower Upham, Upper Lowham, Bishops Waltham, and a few more places besides.

The first sailor, having finished off the rum, got no further than Betty Mundy's Bottom that night, and settled down under the same tree he'd slumbered under all that time ago.

'Well,' said Betty Mundy, appearing in the tree, 'you made a mess of that you gurt lummox. Who has my treasures now, eh? The wicked bloody witch of Stephen's Castle, that's who.'

'Sorry,' said the sailor, 'I'm hungry.'

'Eat a bloody apple then,' said Betty, and looking up the sailor saw an apple tree where there hadn't been one before, and it was groaning under the weight of the juiciest apples you've ever seen.

The sailor picked one, bit into it, and – oh Lord – his nose started to grow. It grew out from his face and then, being too heavy to remain horizontal in the air, clumped to the ground and started to push its way through stinging nettles, brambles and pine needles, whilst Betty Mundy screeched with laughter. It grew its way westwards until it met the Bristol-bound sailor just past Bigpath Farm.

'This is a strange thing,' said he, and followed it back.

The nose then diverted back towards the Meon Valley, meeting the Portsmouth-bound sailor just outside Soberton.

'This is a strange thing,' said he, and followed it back.

As for the nose, it continued down the course of the Meon, through Wickham and Knowle, Catisfield, Titchfield and Little Posbrook, and out into the sea at Hill Head. To the sailor's immense discomfort, it pushed along the seabed, stuffing his nostrils full of wet sand, before it arrived on the Isle of Wight, at Woodside Bay. It pushed its way over the Island, crossing the central ridge at Godshill, before growing down Blackgang Chine, and out into the sea at Chale Bay. Before the nose crossed the Channel to France, Betty relented.

'Give him a pear, boys,' she said, and – lo and behold – there, next to the apple tree, was a pear tree, groaning under the weight of fine-looking pears. As soon as the sailor bit into one of these, his nose started to shrink – faster and faster – till – SLAP – it was back to its normal size (which wasn't small).

'Silly buggers,' said Betty, 'get my treasures back.'

The sailors couldn't work out how this was to be done, so in the end Betty had to tell them.

One sailor (I'd imagine it was the one who favoured Portsmouth) dressed himself as a woman, and, with a basket full of those lovely apples, he presented himself outside the door of Stephen's Castle, crying out in a voice as high as possible, 'Lovely apples! Apples for sale, lovely apples!'

The princess, on seeing the luscious fruit, had another fit of the 'I wants' and bought the apples, after which the transvestite sailor hastened away from the castle as speedily as possible. The princess took a bite from the apple and her nose grew and grew – across her bed chamber, out of the window, and down the castle wall into the moat. Well, with the princess's nose heading for the Continent, the king desperately called for all the physicians in the land to come and save her. So, one of our sailors, dressed as a physician, arrived at the gates of the castle, armed with apples and pears. With a piece of this and a piece of that, and the nose shrinking and growing again, the sailor said, 'There is evil at work here, and you must have stolen goods about you or my cure would surely work.'

The princess denied this at first, but, when the end of her nose encountered a blob fish on the floor of the Solent, she confessed all.

The treasures were restored to the sailors, and the princess got back the nose which was considered so pretty by the tedious people who hung about the castle. As for Betty Mundy, she married all three sailors – seeing how she'd worn out her last three husbands – and they all set up a pub, on a lane, by a wood. This, my dears, is how the lane came to be called Sailor's Lane and the wood Sailor's Wood – just as the bottom had come to be called Betty Mundy's Bottom – and they all lived happily ever after. Sadly, the pub is long gone now – but it used to be one of the best pubs in Hampshire.

THE CHURCH WITH NO NAME

Corhampton, Meonstoke and Exton are so close that nowadays they form one settlement with three churches. As they only have two pubs, this creates a most undesirable imbalance. Many visitors have assumed that St Andrew's Church, Meonstoke, is Corhampton Church, and whilst they have visited a beautiful church, they have missed the real jewel of the Meon Valley. The little graveyard on the mound is part of Corhampton Church's beauty; and there are gravestones in the shadow of the ancient yew tree with evocative names like 'Fortune Coker' and 'Levi and Charity Singleton'. Legend tells of another grave, and I shall tell the story.

At one time, there was a custom in parts of Hampshire to put a fag-hook (the Hampshire phrase for a sickle) on the top of a newly occupied grave. This was to stop the dead from walking; the dead didn't particularly want to walk because it delayed their entry into paradise, so, if the custom was neglected, the dead could get quite upset about it.

Now, on a farm near Corhampton – I don't know which farm – there lived a farmer. He was prosperous and well respected; a local magistrate and altogether a most worthy fellow. It so happens that sometimes a worthy father is let down by his less-than-worthy son, and so it was in this case. The son was an energetic young man, but his energies weren't spent on the farm. Rather, they were spent on gallivanting around at night: poaching, gambling, drinking, and generally keeping bad company. He was also a handsome and rather dashing young man, so the young women liked him, and – oh dear me – didn't he put one of those young women in the family way.

Well, his father got to hear about this and he summoned his recalcitrant son to him, sat him down at the kitchen table, and said, 'Now, if you want to inherit this farm from me, you will have to change your ways. You'll have to stop gallivanting about at night, you'll have to pull your weight on the farm, and you'll have to marry that young woman and make a good husband to her and a good father to the child.'

What the father didn't know was that actually his son was in love with the young woman, and he was going to ask her to marry him. But he was going to ask her to marry him because that's what *he* wanted, not because that's what his father wanted, and – oh dear me – fathers and sons – didn't they fall to arguing, and didn't their fists bang on the table, and didn't the spit fly everywhere.

The long and the short of it was that the son went stamping off out of the house in a red rage, off down the sunken lane. Now, this young man thought he knew every track, every by-way, every sunken lane, between Droxford and East Meon – and yet, when he calmed down and came to his senses, he didn't have a clue where he was. He was at a fork in the lane, and at the fork in the lane there was a withered, blasted, old elm tree. When it's dark, the moonlight and the shadows can play tricks with your vision – but he could swear that leaning against the dead tree there was a coffin, all upended. He approached it, hoping it was just a shadow; but, sure enough, it was a coffin. The young man fumbled at the lid, and opened it like a door. Saints preserve us; inside was the body of an old woman, her arms folded across her withered breasts, and her face wriggling and heaving with maggots and worms. The horror-struck young man slammed the lid shut, and then he heard voices from the left-hand lane. Quick as he could, he hid himself behind an oak tree at the side of the track, and then, out of the darkness, came a host of little men. Now, Cornwall and Devon lay much exaggerated claim to the pixies, but they were always much more active in Hampshire (as can be seen by those stone toadstools on which old Hampshire barns are so often set).

The pixies gathered around the coffin and one of them said, 'We has to bury she proper, loike.'

'Wait, you,' said another, 'someone's been tampering with this.'

'Who would that be then?'

'The gobby young man that can help us bury her.'

And, quick as you like, the pixies were gathered around the young man, who had thought he was all hidden away; their gimlet eyes were glinting in the darkness, and they were saying, 'Give us a hand there, hog face, we needs to bury her.'

'I don't do nothing for no one,' said the young man – and that was his mistake. The pixies were soon on him, dragging him down the lane, with his fingers cutting grooves in the mud. At the foot of the coffin, they grabbed him by the hair, hoisted him to his feet, and opened the lid. Oh dear me – oh dear me – his face was just inches away from that of the corpse, and – SNAP – she opened her eyes. Worse was to come. All of a sudden, she leapt out of the coffin and straight onto his back, with her arms around his neck, and her legs around his waist. A terrible stench enveloped him, a stench that was worse than the baddest bad breath you could ever imagine, and she screeched in his ear, 'FAG-HOOK, FAG-HOOK!'

'Get off me, get off me,' gurgled the young man, trying to scrape her off against a tree. But the more he tried to detach her, the tighter was her grip, and the louder she screeched, 'FAG-HOOK, FAG-HOOK!'

Then, one of the pixies said, 'Here you are my dear,' and handed the old woman a sickle, which she held, ominously, against the young man's throat.

'Bye bye,' said the pixie, and all the little men disappeared off down the lane, leaving the young man and the corpse, lurching around beneath the old elm tree.

Then she hissed in his ear, 'Bury me, bury me.'

'Where?' groaned the young man.

'East Meon,' said she, 'All Saints'.'

'For God's sake, I don't know where I am.'

But … there was a bony finger pointing up the right-hand lane, with the flesh hanging off in strips. So the young man followed the direction shown by the pointing digit; up hill, down dale, through beds of nettles and bramble bushes, across streams and through hedges. Sometimes he knew where he was, sometimes he didn't. There he was on the wild summit of Old Winchester Hill, which is nowhere near Winchester, and then he was in some wretched thicket. Finally, there ahead of them, was All Saints' Church, East Meon.

'Bury me,' hissed the old woman.

'Where?' groaned the young man, stumbling into the grave-yard.

'Inside,' said she.

The young man stumbled up to the porch, but the door was locked. There, though, leaning against the side of the porch, was a spade; so the young man took the spade and levered the door open. There they were inside the old church, and the carvings of Adam and Eve and the Great Serpent seemed to glare at them from the wondrous font. The finger pointed at the flagstones, so the young man levered one aside, and, with the corpse clamped to his back and the fag-hook pressed to his throat, he started to dig. Then the spade sank into something soft, and, oh dear me, wasn't it another corpse of another old woman. She sat up and screamed, 'GET OUT OF YERE, GET BURIED IN YOUR OWN PARISH!'

'Sorry dear,' said the corpse, and ordered the young man to fill the grave up again and replace the flagstones. Stumbling back out into the graveyard, she hissed in his ear again, 'Bury me.'

'Where – please – where?'

'West Meon – St Nicholas' Chapel,' said she.

Now, St Nicholas' Chapel is long gone, though you can still see the ruins opposite Westbury Manor Farm. Maybe it was even a ruin in the time of the story, but who knows what can happen when you're stumbling around the countryside with a corpse on your back and a fag-hook at your throat.

Strangest thing, though. As they approached the church, a fizzling, crackling, wall of lightning seemed to surround it, and when the young man touched it with his spade, the spade was ripped from his hand and hurled up into the sky.

'Bury me,' hissed the corpse again.

'Where?'

'The snowdrop church; Church of Our Lady – Warnford church.'

And, once again, the young man was staggering through streams and thickets and copses; and there was the Church of Our Lady, and there were all the graves opening, and there were all the bodies poking their heads out of the graves – and all of them screeching, 'Go away, go away, get buried in your own parish!'

'Oh all right,' said the old woman, 'take me home.'

'Where?' whispered the young man, with barely any breath left in his body.

'Corhampton,' she said, 'The church with no name.'

And so, as the first grey light of dawn showed above the chalk hills, and the birds started to sing in the trees, they

finally approached old Corhampton Church – and there was a freshly dug grave. And, sticking in the pile of earth next to it, at a crazy angle, was the spade – it must have been where it landed. The young man staggered towards the grave, and there, inside, was an open coffin, of a most luxurious construction.

'Ooooh, very nice,' said the corpse, and in a flash she was lying in the coffin, with her arms crossed, and the fag-hook in one hand.

'Take the fag-hook then, and bury me,' she said to the young man as he gawped into the hole in stupefaction. So he took the sickle, and fastened the coffin. He shovelled the earth back into the hole, and finally laid the sickle on the top of the grave. Well, after this he stumbled home, covered in cuts and bruises, with his clothes in shreds.

I gather that he did marry the young woman, and that he was a responsible husband and father. Maybe, just maybe, he was a little bit of a disappointment to his new wife; she had, after all, fallen in love with the dashing young ne'er do well – but such a man doesn't make a good husband. He never did want to go out at night again, though.

So, if you ever visit Corhampton Church, and I recommend that you do, be careful when you cross the graveyard – just in case the corpse fancies moving again.

OLD WINCHESTER HILL

Old Winchester Hill, like Corhampton Church, is one of the
wonders of Hampshire. The name is deceptive, because it is
eleven miles from Winchester; it gazes across the Meon Valley
towards Beacon Hill, one of the two Beacon Hills of Hampshire.
When the Iron Age hill fort on the top had ramparts, with chalk
sides which shone brilliant white in the sun, it must have been
a commanding sight.

One of the stories explaining the name of the hill says that
the Romans wanted to build their regional capital, Winchester,
on the top; but every night the stones were rolled down to the
bottom. Finally the Romans gave up, building their city along
the River Itchen, and ever after avoided the cursed Meon. It is
interesting that in a county with a lot of Roman remains, there
is very little evidence of Roman habitation along the Meon
Valley.

The view from the top is wondrous; on a clear day you can
see for miles. Sometimes, though, on a misty day, you can see
barely a few yards ahead, and the old thorn tree looms out of
the mist like a guardian of the hill.

There are many stories of ghosts and spectres on the top of
the hill, and I've felt the presence of others when I thought I
was alone; I have seen figures, and then lost them from sight.
I tend to blame this on the workings of my imagination, but
it's not surprising that other people's imaginations work in the
same way on this singular hill.

There is a story that, on a misty day, a line of warriors on
horseback can be seen trooping across the hill – silently
out of the mist before being swallowed up again – and that
their faces are ancient and care-worn. I was told that this apparition related to the story of a king who had feasted under the
hill. I was never given a name of this king, but I came across
a nearly identical story that was set in some non-geographical

space, a never-never land, and that the name of the king was
Herla. To me, being a literal sort of a person, there is no inner
landscape without outer landscape – so I can only assume that
the story took place on Old Winchester Hill!

Once upon a time, when all of Hampshire was deeply
wooded, when all the fragments we have now – the New
Forest, Corhampton Forest, the Forest of Bere, Alice Holt
Forest, Lordswood, Southleigh Forest, Harewood Forest,
Pamber Forest and the rest – were part of the wildwood,
there was a king called Herla. One day, Herla was riding upon
the hill; he was hunting the deer, or maybe it was the wild
boar. As he ascended the ramparts of Old Winchester Hill, a
little man with a beard that was longer than he was himself
approached, riding on a goat.

'You are a great king, and an even better hunter,' said the little
man (this was a compliment), 'and if I can come to your wedding, you can come to mine.'

'Right you are,' said the king. The little man promptly sank
into the hill.

Not long afterwards, the king took a wife. She was a radiant
beauty, nearly as beautiful as Betty Mundy. At the wedding feast,
the little man came into the great hall, riding on a goat. Behind
him was a whole host of little people, bearing wondrous gifts:
cups and drinking horns, roast hogs on spits, pies so delicious
that the eating of them made your toes curl, and barrels of the
most delicious ale.

'I'll have a drop of this,' said Herla.

'You're welcome,' said the little man, 'but don't forget you're
coming to my bash too.'

'Wouldn't miss it for the world,' said the king.

The next year, the king received word that the little man was
about to get hitched, so he took his most faithful warriors and
rode off to Old Winchester Hill. When he was on the top, a

mist rolled in from the sea, up the valley, and over the hill – and Herla and his warriors found themselves sinking into the ground, into a mighty feasting hall. The King under the Hill was there with his fairy bride, and there were tables laden with pies and cheeses, and pork with crackling, and cider and beer that was so good it made your eyes roll up in your head and the belches come bursting forth in a fashion most royal.

So they feasted and drank for three days and three nights. Before they left, the King under the Hill gave Herla the gift of a bloodhound, and told him not to dismount from his horse until the bloodhound jumped to the ground. The king rode out onto the hill and the forests were gone. There was a yew wood and a beech wood; the king rode between them. There were fields in the valley and the strange sound of tolling bells. King Herla rode down the valley and all seemed strange. He approached an old man with a flock of sheep, and the king asked, 'Where is my kingdom, the Kingdom of Herla?'

The old man spoke to him in a fractured version of his own tongue. He told him that the Kingdom of Herla was the stuff of legends, and that since that alleged time the Jutes had rowed up the river, and a canting saint called Wilfrid had come to the valley at the head of a rich entourage during a time of hunger, and churches had been built and the forest cut down. One of the king's men then tried to dismount – but as his feet touched the ground, he crumbled into dust. Since then, King Herla has ridden Old Winchester Hill waiting for the day that the blood-hound leaps to the ground – but that day is still to come.

Six

WINCHESTER

Once upon a time, I was due to tell some stories in Winchester City Museum. Before doing so, I tried to imagine myself in medieval Winchester. I found this quite difficult; Winchester is a tidy and prosperous town, average earnings there are nearly twice as much as those on the western edge of Southampton, and it was difficult for me to translate this into a teeming medieval city.

That year, I went to a wedding in Amritsar, capital of the Indian Punjab. Amritsar is the centre of Sikhism; it contains the sacred and wondrous Golden Temple. As my companions and I walked through the narrow streets and alleys of old Amritsar, we felt ourselves drawing closer to the holy temple. The sound of the *kirtan* chanted out from the temple grew louder, the crowds of people increased, and the sound and feeling of approaching somewhere special almost seemed to vibrate through our feet from the ground. Then we rounded the corner and there was the Golden Temple – and my heart missed a beat. Crowds were streaming in and out, there were guards and holy men, hawkers and vendors, worshippers and pilgrims, and above all of this was the sound of devotional chanting. I felt that I was at the centre of something vast.

Then it occurred to me – here was medieval Winchester. People from the country winding their way through narrow streets, many of them having never seen buildings on the scale of those found in the city. Then, as pilgrims to the shrine of St Swithun approached the cathedral, they might have heard the monks reciting the liturgy of the hours, or singing vespers and then, rounding a corner in an alleyway, there, looming above them, the vast, wondrous cathedral. Nowadays the cathedral is a wondrous sight – how much more so to medieval eyes? So this city – Alfred's capital, capital of Wessex, original capital of the ancient Kingdom of England – is stuffed full of stories, and the border between myth and history can become very blurred.

King Alfred is forever associated with Winchester – as his statue, dominating the eastern end of The Broadway, insists on reminding us. Alfred, whilst being an historical figure, has morphed into legend, as has William Rufus. Once upon a time, everyone knew the story of Alfred and the burnt cakes, though I'm not sure that they do now.

The king who is always associated with myth and legend, however, is Arthur; and Arthur is also associated with Winchester. Winchester is one of the several places given as the site of Camelot. To me, searching for the actual site of Camelot is a futile activity, as is searching for an actual Arthur. To do so is to misunderstand the way stories morph and merge, and the way one legendary figure can represent many historical figures, and many things.

Winchester also lays claim to Arthur's round table, and the table top is a spectacular sight, hanging in Winchester's Great Hall. The table was actually created for Edward I in the late thirteenth century, and painted in its present way for Henry VIII in the sixteenth century – all kings wanted to give themselves an Arthurian pedigree. It is significant, though, that the table is located in Winchester, and not London.

And then there is Sleepers Hill. All over the country there are said to be warriors and other worlds located under hills – something we have already encountered under Old Winchester Hill. The story of Arthur under the hill is claimed by Craig y Dinas in Gwynedd, Alderney Edge in Cheshire, and many more. Indeed, there are sleeping warriors under many hills in many countries; I even encountered one in Gran Canaria, where a Guanchero chieftain is said to sleep under El Roque Nublo!

I only know of one hill, though, that takes its name from the legend, and that is Sleepers Hill in Winchester. I therefore make no apology for including the legend of …

Sleepers Hill

It looks rather expensive now – a private road, large houses – very Winchester; but it wasn't always so. It used to be outside the city, a city which nestles in a dip in the hills around the River Itchen. Down by the river there are water meadows, and at one time there was marshland beyond the meadows. No one lived there because there were insects that could give you agues and fevers: well, not exactly no one – there was one person. This was an old woman who lived in a rickety-rackety wooden hut; some people called her a wise woman and some people called her a witch. The people who called her a wise woman were the people who lived thereabouts, and they treated her like a doctor. If their rheumatism was playing them up they'd visit her for some lotions or potions, or if the baby was ill they'd visit her for some herbs or tinctures. The people who called her a witch, however – well, usually they were the richer people, and they were the people who wanted something. Maybe they wanted a love potion to make someone fall in love with them, or maybe they wanted a spell to make them even richer than they already were.

There was a young man like that, and he was already rich. Well, strictly speaking he wasn't rich, his father was. His father was a Winchester merchant and landowner, and he kept his son in great style. The young man had servants, fine food and drink, and an allowance that he could gamble away – but the father knew that the son was foolish with money, so he wasn't getting his hands on the family fortune. The son didn't like that; 'It's not fair' was his refrain. So he thought he'd go and see the wise old woman of the marshes.

The moon was rising up into the sky when he trudged out to the rickety-rackety wooden hut. He knocked on the door. There was a grumbling and shuffling from inside, the door creaked open, and there was the old woman.

'What do you want?' she demanded, her expression hostile.

'I want a spell, witch.'

'Oh, do you indeed? Well, come inside.'

He went inside and sat down by the fire. 'I want a…' he began.

'BE QUIET!' she shrieked – and he had to sit there for what seemed an age, gazing into the flames. From within the flames there were warning pictures of treasure and death. Eventually, the woman spoke: 'Well, what is it? What do you want?'

'I want a spell to make me rich, and I'll pay you well for it.' Well, he'd be able to if he was rich!

'Ah, do you? Do you know Sleepers Hill?'

'Yes, yes.'

'Do you know the stories? About Arthur and the sleeping warriors?'

'Stories – a lot of old nonsense, for children. I hate children; horrible smelly things.'

'Oh, indeed. Well, I'll tell you. Underneath that hill there is treasure – gold and silver for the taking.'

He was listening now, because she had said 'treasure'.

'Come back tomorrow morning and bring with you a lantern and a strong spade.'

The next morning, at the crack of dawn (he'd never got up so early in his life before), he was back with a strong spade. Up they went to Sleepers Hill; they walked three times round the hill, and then up to the top.

'Can you see it?' she asked, 'Can you see a hazel tree?'

No – there was nothing.

'Wait now', she said, 'and I'll play a tune on my magic pipe.' She produced a strange little wooden flute from one of her many pockets, and played a tune that was either tuneless or tuneful; a tune that sounded like the wind in the grass on the chalk downs. There, in front of them, was a hazel tree. It hadn't appeared in a puff of smoke; it was as if it had always been there, but something had gone from their eyes and allowed them to see.

'Take the spade,' she ordered, 'and dig it up.'

So he took the spade and dug and dug. This was hard, because there's always a tap root that goes down further than the others, and he was not used to hard work. Eventually, he dragged the tree out of the ground, and there, underneath, was a rock.

'Shift it,' the woman said.

So the young man heaved and hoed and eventually shifted it to one side. There was a dark tunnel, leading deep into the hill. Lifting the lantern, and with the old woman behind him, down he went into the tunnel. The first thing he saw, hanging from the roof of the tunnel, was a bell.

'Don't touch that bell,' she hissed, 'if you do, you'll waken the sleeping warriors. Now, if by some terrible mischance you do waken the sleeping warriors, they will say, "Is it time?"

If this happens, you must say, "No, it is not yet time, sleep thou on".'

But the young man wasn't listening, because all he wanted was treasure, and already he was further down the tunnel. The next thing he saw was a cold bluey-green flame. There were some logs, but the logs weren't burning. The flame flickered above them and gave off a little bit of light, but no warmth. Then he was in a huge, round cavern with a vaulted ceiling, and there was a terrible sight. Lying on the ground was Arthur, dressed in a full suit of armour, with the visor pulled back from his face – and his face was as pale as death itself. Around him, lying in a circle, were all the knights of the round table: Galahad, Lancelot, Gawaine, Percival, Lyonell, Trystram, Gareth, Bedivere, Blioberis, Lacotemale, Lucane, Palomedes, Lamorak, Bors, Saphar, Pellinore, Kay, Ector, Dagonet, Degore, Brunar, Guinglain, Alymore and Mordred. Quite what Mordred, the cause of Arthur's downfall, was doing there, I don't know – but I can only go by the knights on the Winchester Round Table!

There, in the middle of the terrible circle, was treasure: a pile of gold and a pile of silver. 'Money – money – money,' thought the young man, his eyes gleaming. He regretted now not having a sack, but he stuffed as much gold as he could down his clothes. Staggering out of the cave, with the weight of the gold, he couldn't walk straight – and, oh dear me, he hit the bell. It rang out, clear and loud. Slowly – slowly – Arthur sat up, his eyes opening and shining in the darkness.

'Is it time? Is it time?' he rasped.

Then, all the other knights started to sit up – 'Is it time? IS IT TIME? IS IT TIME?'

'Help, old woman, what do I say?' screeched the young man.

'You say, "No, it is not yet time, sleep thou on."'

'NO, IT IS NOT YET TIME, SLEEP THOU ON.'

Slowly, their eyes shut and they lay back down again, whilst the young man legged it down the passageway and out into the sunshine on the side of the hill.

'I'm rich, I'm rich!' he shouted, dancing in delight, and then, turning to the old woman, he gave her two of the smallest coins he had.

She muttered and mumbled and went stamping off to her shack in the marshes – but the young man didn't care, he was rich.

He went back to Winchester and bought himself friends. There was drinking and gambling and loose living! He thought of going to London, but then, wasn't Winchester grander than London? And wasn't it the rightful capital of England? Soon the money was all gone – but so what? Wasn't there plenty more where that came from?

Firstly, he went to the old woman's hut. But he didn't go to see the old woman – he waited until she was out. In those days, the poor didn't lock their doors – partly because they couldn't afford locks, and partly because there was usually nothing to steal. The young man ransacked the shack and he *did* find something to steal, for there, under a pile of rags, was the little flute.

He stole the flute, and off he went to Sleepers Hill. One –
two – three times round the hill he went, then up to the top.
There was no hazel tree, and he didn't know how to play a
pipe, but when he lifted it to his lips it seemed to play itself;
it made the sound of distant thunder over the downs. There
was the hazel tree, and once again he dug and dug. Once again
there was the stone, and once again there was the dark tunnel.
Holding the lantern high, down he went into the dark, dark
tunnel.

There was the bell – he was very careful not to touch that
– there was the cold bluey-green flame, and there were the
warriors, lying in a circle. In the circle there was still plenty of
gold, and there was all the silver. This time, the young man had
brought with him a big sack, so he loaded the sack with treasure
and stumbled towards the passageway. It's hard carrying a sack of
treasure, though, and the lantern was bumping against his arm
and burning it – and he stumbled against the bell. Crystal clear,
it rang out across the cavern.

'Is it time?' said Arthur.

'Is it time?' said Galahad.

Then they were all roaring, as they sat upright, their eyes
shining like lanterns in the darkness.

'IS IT TIME? IS IT TIME?'

'Oh God, I know what to say,' thought the panic-stricken
young man – but sometimes something just goes right out of
your head. This is worse, of course, if you're a bit nervous – and
he wasn't a bit nervous, he was terrified. Just then, there was a
screaming, and a neighing, and a whinnying, and there was the
great white head of a horse with a black star on its forehead.
There was no body and no legs (though there was the sound of
clattering hooves) – just the head.

Then the knights started to whirl in a circle – faster and
faster – whirling around the cavern. Arthur himself stepped
out of the whirling circle, drew his great, shining sword

Excalibur, and started to beat the young man with the flat of the sword. Rough hands grabbed hold of him, and he was hurled against one side of the cave, and then the other, backwards and forwards, till, bones broken and unconscious, he was hurled out onto the hillside.

When he came to, and looked around, there was no sign of any cave, no hazel tree, no flute (he'd left that in the cave), and no treasure.

Now, some of the old books in the Hampshire Records Office in Winchester tell a story of how, in Tudor times, a man dressed in rags and tatters used to walk round and round Sleepers Hill, babbling some strange story about sleeping warriors and buried treasure, and I reckon that must have been the young man.

If you ever go to Sleepers Hill, you might stand at the top looking out over old Winchester – though it is advisable not to stand in the middle of the B3040, because you might get run over by a lorry. If, however, instead of looking out over Winchester you look down at your feet, there, still, way down below you, are sleeping warriors and buried treasure.

On the side of the hill is Winchester University, formerly King Alfred's Teacher Training College. There are some great teachers coming out of this place, and I've told this story there. I do hope that some of those teachers tell the story to their pupils, because a told story beats an interactive whiteboard any day!

ORFEO AND THE KING UNDER TWYFORD DOWN

Winchester is a very royal sort of a place; and, what with Arthur and Alfred, it does like its kings. At one time it had a king called Orfeo – at least, it did so according to an anonymous Middle English narrative poem, a poem that merged aspects of Greek mythology with English folklore, and then entered into the oral tradition.

King Orfeo had a wife called Heurodis. One drowsy summer's day, she fell asleep under an apple tree; maybe it was the Apple Tree Man himself. She was surrounded by the buzzing of bees and the droning of insects, and her mind filled with the soft, heavy, juicy, cidery vapours of the apple tree. (The apples that were to grow on the tree in the autumn were proper, juicy, sweet, Hampshire apples, as this was long before Hampshire was invaded by supermarkets and Golden Delicious apples that taste of cardboard.)

In her languid sleep, she dreamed that the King under the Hill came riding up to her on his goat, and the eyes of both king and goat were glittering. He instructed her to sleep under the tree on the following day. The next day, she was drawn back to the tree, but she took a group of armed knights to guard her. Armed knights are no use, though, against the King under the Hill, and though no one saw her disappear, disappear she did.

Orfeo was distraught, and, taking only his harp, he left the court at Winchester to search for his beloved Heurodis. He wandered the greenwood and the high downs; his hair and beard grew long and straggly, and he became a mad, feral, green king, like Nebuchadnezzar before him, sleeping amidst the ferns and bracken, living on roots and bark and mushrooms and berries.

Seven years passed, till, one day, as Orfeo slept in the greenwood near Ovington, in between the River Itchen and Lovington Lane, he was awoken by silvery voices. Peeping from between the leaves, he saw a host of fairy ladies riding by the river, and at their head was Heurodis, a great hawk upon her glove. Picking up his harp, Orfeo followed them as they rode past Avington and Itchen Abbas, Couch Green and Martyr Worthy, until they reached the flank of Twyford

Down, close by Winchester. As they rode up the slope they sank into it, and, as Orfeo followed them, he too sank into the slope, and there he was in the kingdom under the hill, the otherworld. There was no sign of the fairy host, but ahead of him was a wondrous crystal castle, and there was the gatekeeper.

'Hold,' said the gatekeeper, 'who are you?'

'Orfeo, king of the greenwood, walker of the high downs, eater of berries and roots, cousin to the wild boar and the badger.'

'Then you are expected.'

Orfeo entered the castle, and there, all around him, were the bodies of all those who had died and he had known in life. Some were burned, some were wet from drowning, and some were without their heads. Then Orfeo saw Heurodis amongst the bodies, lying as if still asleep under the apple tree.

'You trespass,' said the King under the Hill, sitting astride his goat.

'I seek my queen,' replied Orfeo, 'and I bring my harp.'

'Then play for me,' said the King under the Hill, who could never resist a good tune.

Orfeo played, and as he played the songs of the woods and the wind in the trees, the songs of the larks and the wind over the high downs, the King under the Hill was enraptured.

'Never have I heard such music,' he said, 'choose anything for a reward.'

Orfeo, of course, chose Heurodis, and, as the King under the Hill had given his word, there was nothing he could do about it. So Orfeo and the now fully awake Heurodis returned to Winchester.

To Winchester he is y-come,
That was his owhen cité,
Ach no man knewe that it was he.

Orfeo was unrecognisable, with his ragged clothes and unkempt hair and beard. Leaving Heurodis at a lodging house, he made his way to the Great Hall. On his way, he was insulted and abused by many of the puffed up and pretentious citizens of Winchester, who had no time for raggedy beggars. However, when he arrived at the Great Hall, his old steward recognised the harp. The steward didn't recognise Orfeo, and when he questioned him about the harp, Orfeo tested the steward's loyalty by telling him that he had found the harp next to the mutilated corpse of a man gored to death by a wild boar. The steward collapsed in grief and distress, and so Orfeo began to play the harp, and at once the old steward knew who it was.

Well, after this, Heurodis came to the Great Hall, and the king and queen resumed their reign. So – all well and good – all living happily ever after. Until, that is, 1993–94, when a huge gash was cut through Twyford Down to make way for the M3. In 1992, protesters calling themselves Dongas had occupied the site, but in December they were violently evicted by Group 4 security guards. This day has since been known as Yellow Wednesday, on account of the hi-viz jackets of the guards.

Besides cutting through two Sites of Special Scientific Interest, two Scheduled Ancient Monuments and an Area of Outstanding Natural Beauty, the motorway also cut through the kingdom of the King under the Hill. Since then, it has been claimed that, every so often, a car just disappears from the M3 whilst passing through the Twyford Down cutting; but, as I've never counted them in and counted them out, I can't vouch for the truth of this.

Tales of St Swithun

And if any church fell down, or was in decay, S. Swithun would anon amend it at his own cost. Or if any church were not hallowed, he would thither afoot and hallow it. For he loved no pride, ne to ride on gay horses, ne to be praised ne flattered of the people…

So states *The Golden Legend*, a medieval book of saints' stories. We know little, historically, of St Swithun, except that he was made Bishop of Winchester in 852. He has entered folklore, however, as a generous and otherworldly saint, living in a time of great turbulence, and the stories about him are homely and humble. The turbulent times were described by the thirteenth-century historian Roger de Hoveden:

Nothing was deemed disgraceful except piety, while innocence was considered most deserving of a violent death. In consequence, the Lord Almighty, sent down upon them, like swarms of bees, most bloodthirsty nations, who spared neither age nor sex, such as the Danes and Goths, the Norwegians and Swedes, the Vandals and the Frisians.

This hideous crew of North Europeans laid the country to waste, and when a force of Saxons defeated the Danes at Southampton, the Danes took their revenge a few years later. Refreshing, then, to find a saint who is constructive – and Swithun was; he was a bridge builder. Prayer and meditation are worthwhile activities, but a bit of engineering always separates the practical saints from the rest.

Swithun and the Eggs

Swithun was building a bridge over the River Itchen, at the bottom of Winchester High Street. One day, he was down at

the bridge; some stories say he was preaching there, others that
he was blessing the bridge, but I prefer to think that he was carrying out a health and safety inspection. A large crowd gathered
– workmen and passers-by – and they had the manners and lack
of care of people living in a violent time. An old woman passed
by, carrying a basket of eggs, and this was all the food she had
in the world. The old soul was jostled by the uncaring crowd,
and the basket fell to the ground, smashing all the eggs. The dis-
tressed old woman tried to retrieve her basket, but the crowd
continued to jostle her.

On the bridge, Swithun let out a roar: 'SILENCE!' and the
crowd was stilled. He strode through the mass of people and
up to the old woman. Then he knelt down in front of her
and began to pick up the eggshells; as he did so the eggs were
miraculously restored, and it was a basket of whole eggs that he
returned to the old woman.

This is a little miracle (though maybe not to the old
woman), but it represents an act of humanity in an inhumane
time. It is a small story, but an important one. This is one of
the two stories about St Swithun that have been uncov-

ered as wall paintings in Corhampton Church, and that little church seems almost more appropriate to Swithun than the mighty Winchester Cathedral. There is, however, a church dedicated to St Swithun above Winchester's Kingsgate. It seems rather apt that the church incorporates a bridge.

Swithun and the Weather

Most of the stories about miracles associated with Swithun seem to take place after his death. Before he died, Swithun made it clear that he didn't want to be buried in the cathedral, but outside, where his body would be subject to the feet of passers-by and the raindrops that fell from on high. Some years later, it was decided to move the body inside, and the saint marked his displeasure by summoning up a downpour which soaked everyone to the skin. He has been forever after associated with the rain and weather.

St Swithun's day if thou dost rain
For forty days it will remain
St Swithun's day if thou be fair
For forty days 'twill rain nae mare

St Swithun's Day is 15 July and would have been important in the agricultural calendar; the state of the weather for forty days after this date would have a great impact on the harvest.

Swithun and the Wild Women

Now we come to the other story about St Swithun that is pictured on the wall of Corhampton Church: a young man came to Winchester from the countryside; he was innocent and unused to the ways of the wicked city. As he crossed Swithun's Bridge at the bottom of the High Street, two wild women approached him (something still quite likely to happen nowadays). In terror – and I know how he feels – the young man fell back against the parapet. The wild women continued to approach him, screaming obscenities and waving their undergarments – and the young man toppled into the river and was drowned. The body was dragged from the Itchen and carried to the shrine of St Swithun. Swithun felt sorry for the poor yokel, and he was restored to life. The young man returned to his village, bearing tales of loose women and miraculous restorations to life; he was probably never short of a free drink after that.

Swithun and the Nine Plough Shares

St Swithun could be called on to help when necessary. In the eleventh century, he helped Queen Emma out of a very awkward situation. Emma had married her second husband, the hideous Cnut, in order to consolidate and make safe the kingdom. They produced a son called Edward, who became king after the death of Cnut, though not directly so. As always, lots of plotting and politicking was going on. Robert, Archbishop of Canterbury, poisoned the ears of the king. Forty-eight years after the death of her first husband, and fifteen years after the death of Cnut, Robert whispered into the ears of the king that Emma, his mother, had been having a fling with Aelfwine, Bishop of Winchester. She is 'a wild thing, not a woman', he hissed. Oh dear me – she would have to walk the nine burning plough shares. This meant that nine plough shares would be heated till red hot and placed in the nave of Winchester Cathedral – and the queen was to walk them.

A throng of people flocked to the cathedral to goggle and ogle; the queen was stripped of her shoes and stockings, she lay aside her mantle, put off her veil, drew her garments about her, and in between two bishops she was brought to the plough shares. The queen kept her head held high, but the two bishops wept, 'Oh, St Swithun, St Swithun, help her,' and there, seen only to the eyes of the queen and walking ahead of her, was St Swithun, as impatient as he always was with fools and power-hungry plotters. She walked the nine plough shares, and not a single burn did she receive.

Edward cast himself at his mother's feet and most justly received a good whacking from both his mum and the Bishop of Winchester. As for the Archbishop of Canterbury, he'd fled to Normandy before they could lay hands on him.

STRAIGHTFORWARD WORK

There may be lots of medieval folklore surrounding Winchester Cathedral, but a more recent event has been so singular that it has passed into legend. This event is the long, drawn-out labours of William Walker, something that Walker himself described as '…not difficult. It was straightforward work, but had to be carefully done'. William Walker was a diver, and he saved the cathedral from sinking into the ground.

The cathedral was built on peat, and was always in danger of collapse – indeed, the tower fell down in either 1101 or 1107, something that was always blamed on Rufus the Red, because

his wicked bones had been buried there. In the early twentieth century, the cathedral was slowly sinking into the peat, and in order to make it possible for bricklayers to build supporting walls, the groundwater had to be lowered – under normal circumstances this would cause the cathedral to collapse. Someone had to submerge themselves under the peaty water, and, working in pitch darkness, shore up the walls.

This was William Walker, who had started his diving career in the murky waters of Portsmouth Dockyard. From 1906 until 1911 he worked six hours a day, and at weekends cycled 150 miles home to Croydon and back, to see his family. During this time, he used more than 25,000 bags of concrete, 115,000 concrete blocks, and 900,000 bricks. He saved the cathedral. When his work was done, the groundwater was pumped out and the bricklayers could do their work.

In 1912, to celebrate the completion of the task, a thanksgiving service was held in the cathedral (which remained standing). King George V presented Walker with a rose bowl. This was the second time they had met, because it was William Walker who had taught George how to dive when the future king was a naval cadet.

This is history; stuff that definitely happened. Sometimes, though, history is also folklore. This is because William Walker, diver, is a legend.

Seven

THE TEST VALLEY

As Winchester has its magnificent cathedral, so Romsey has its magnificent abbey. This grew from a religious community originally established in 907 at Rum's Eg. Rum's Eg means a raised piece of land in the marshes, the marshes of the River Test, and this became shortened to Romsey. Romsey lies at the southern end of the Test Valley, and south of Romsey the River Test flows down to Southampton Water, where, with the River Itchen, it creates the Southampton peninsula. The community at Romsey had built an abbey, which was burnt down by another ghastly group of Danish Vikings. The current great abbey was built around the year 1000.

Nuns didn't always become nuns through religious vocation; convents were places of social control. The daughters of nobility could be sent there until they were married off for political convenience, or, if they weren't to be married, they could take holy orders and stay there. From outside they could be seen, by the controlling men, in an almost erotic way – as in this rather Freudian description of Romsey Abbey, by the obviously overheated and sweaty

Archbishop Peckham in 1283:

In a lily garden the Bridegroom is filled with delight, and finds pleasure in gathering lilies above all other flowers. It is therefore needful to enclose this garden by the defence of shrewd and sharp discipline, as the Paradise of God was enclosed by angelic care and the flaming sword, lest an entrance be opened to the serpent into the same, or to any sower of mischief, by which the pleasure of the Bridegroom should be turned to displeasure or less liking.

So nunneries could be prisons, protecting women from the sowers of mischief. In Romsey, however, on occasion the nuns seemed to take control. In the fourteenth century, Abbess Alicia de Wyntereshulle was murdered by poison, and the subsequent investigation found the whole convent – abbess, nuns, officials and servants – guilty of scandalous living.

In the fifteenth century, Abbess Elizabeth Broke confessed to perjury and committing adultery with one John Placy. She resigned, but was promptly re-elected. Later, enquiries found that she was more than friendly with the Reverend Bryce, the chaplain of the infirmary, and that the nuns slipped out at night and frequented the taverns, and that some of them slept in the less desirable houses of the town. It was also suggested that Abbess Elizabeth and Reverend Bryce had a daughter. None of this seemed to be an excuse to throw Elizabeth Broke out of her position, because she continued as abbess until her natural death.

The story that has entered folklore, however, is of one of the early abbesses, Ethelfleda, and her life was entirely without moral stain – wasn't it?

ETHELFLEDA OF RUM'S EG

Ethelfleda's stepfather was Edgar the Peaceful. He was so peaceful that he murdered Ethelfleda's father Ethelwold in Harewood Forest so that he could take his wife. This is a story we will come to shortly. Edgar married the newly made widow Elfrida and decided to dispose of her unwanted daughter by sending her to Romsey Abbey. The abbess was a saintly Irish woman called Morwenna, and she became like a mother to Ethelfleda. Ethelfleda, herself, soon became known for saintliness; it was said that her fingertips could give off light, so she could read the scriptures at night – and she seemed to be quite busy during the night.

One day, her teacher went out into a plantation of saplings to cut switches. There was nothing this teacher liked more than beating the young women with switches, beating the fear of God into them. Ethelfleda miraculously saw through the stone wall of the abbey (cynics have said that she just followed the mistress) and she saw the sadistic woman cut the switches and hide them in her dress. When the teacher re-entered the building, Ethelfleda cast herself at her feet and cried, 'Do not, mistress, beat us with the switches: we will sing and chant at your pleasure.' The mistress thought that the Holy Spirit had told the girl, and thereafter lived in fear of the saintly Ethelfleda, never beating any of the young women again.

Then the queen came to stay at Romsey, to be looked after by the nuns. The queen noticed that Ethelfleda had a habit of disappearing at night-time, so one night she decided to follow. In the darkness she lost sight of the young woman, but then in the moonlight she saw Ethelfleda standing naked by the crystal-clear waters of the River Test. There was no one else in sight – certainly not, how could there be? No one hastily disappearing into the undergrowth. Ethelfleda noticed the queen and leaped into the cold water, where she began chanting Davidian psalms. The queen fainted, and was later told that Ethelfleda was so saintly that she made a habit of standing in the freezing waters of the Test at night, singing praises to God. Thereafter the queen took Ethelfleda to be the holiest of holy women, which suited Ethelfleda just fine.

After the death of Morwenna, though not directly after, Ethelfleda became abbess. She continued with her saintly habits. One time, a bailiff placed his rent money in the care of the abbess, and, oh dear me, it all disappeared. She bowed her head and apologised for the fact that her care and compassion for the poor was so great that she just had to spend it on them. She said that if he waited a while, she was sure it would be miraculously restored. Then it was restored – most of it, well, some of it, after a while.

I believe that Romsey still has its strange goings-on, and wanderings at night, but I wouldn't want to listen to tittle tattle, for isn't gossip just something for idle minds?

DEADMAN'S PLACK

If we wander north of Romsey, we can follow the Test Valley. It's a gorgeous wander up through King's Somborne, Stockbridge and Chilbolton. To follow the River Test itself can be bewildering. Brian Vesey-Fitzgerald writes:

The Test does all sorts of extraordinary things: it is now broad, quite a mighty river, it is now narrow, divides and divides again, is now two streams, now one, now three – so that I am never certain whether I am following the parent stream or some wayward child.

If we continue northwards along the Test we come to Wherwell, and Harewood Forest. We have already heard about the murder of Ethelfleda's father, Ethelwold, in this forest, and should you go walking there you might come across a monument called Deadman's Plack. On the monument is the following inscription:

About the year of our Lord DCCCCLXIII (ad 963) upon this spot beyond the time of memory called Deadman's Plack, tradition reports that Edgar, surnamed the peaceable [sic], King of England, in the ardour of youth love and indignation, slew with his own hand his treacherous and ungrateful favourite Earl Athelwold, owner of this forest of Harewood, in resentment of the Earl's having basely betrayed and perfidiously married his intended bride and beauteous Elfrida, daughter of Ordgar, Earl of Devonshire, afterwards wife of King Edgar, and by him mother of King Ethelred II, Queen Elfrida, after Edgar's death, murdered his eldest son, King Edward the Martyr, and founded the Nunnery of Wor-well

It portrays Edgar the Peaceful as a wronged hero, but all stories can be seen from different points of view. I'll begin my 'Once upon a time' with Ordgar, Earl of Devonshire. Ordgar had a daughter called Elfrida, and she was renowned for her beauty. These feuding, Mafia-like, royal families bartered their daughters like commodities, and the women had to develop strong powers of cunning and manipulation if they themselves were to survive their own manipulation.

King Edgar the Peaceful was a swaggerer, and to impress the men at court he cut a notch in his belt for every woman he had sex with. Given that he was king, it was a very dangerous thing to say no, even though he displayed all the charm of a Tamworth ginger pig. The king got to hear about Elfrida, and so he sent his friend Ethelwold down to darkest Devon to have a look for himself. Ethelwold was Ealdorman for Hampshire, a high-ranking official, and being Ealdorman for

Hampshire was an important post, given that the king was in Winchester. Ethelwold was told that if Elfrida lived up to her reputation, he was to bring her back to the court.

Ethelwold took the long road down to Devon – and when he met Elfrida he was smitten. Elfrida found herself being courted by the Ealdorman of Hampshire, and, given that he neglected to mention the original purpose of his mission, she thought she'd got a pretty good catch. Ethelwold sent word back to Winchester that Elfrida actually looked like a cross between a hobgoblin and a pigsie, and promptly married her himself.

Ethelwold and Elfrida settled down in the now defunct manor of Easington-Dacre, on the wet and wild flank of Dartmoor, and Ethelwold was very happy. Elfrida, however, was tired of dark and dreary Devon and longed for the glamour of the court. Edgar had moved on to other conquests, but rumours started to reach Winchester that his friend, the Ealdorman of Hampshire, had acquired a beautiful wife, and Edgar began to wonder why he'd never returned. So he sent a messenger down to Easington-Dacre, and demanded the presence of husband and wife at court. Now Ethelwold's heart sank into his boots, and his neck began to itch, just along the chopping point. He entreated his beautiful wife to dress as badly as possible, in filthy old sacks, and to smear her face with cow dung and pig bristles.

Once at the court in Winchester, Ethelwold and Edgar embraced, and drank from the drinking horn. Then the king said, 'You must introduce me to your wife.'

The woman who stepped forth into the presence of the king was no pigsie-bristle, but a beauty, attired in the most desirable and provocative way, and whose movements were so sinuous, that different parts of her anatomy seemed to be moving in different directions at the same time. The king's eyes popped out of his head, and lust, combined with rage at

Ethelwold's deception, formed a most unpleasant cocktail in his mind.

Edgar 'dissembled his indignation', as chronicler William of Malmesbury put it, and took Ethelwold hunting in Harewood Forest. Deep in the forest, he ran his former friend through with a javelin, and left him choking his life away amongst the trees. Maybe the hunting expedition was Elfrida's idea, and she was certainly far too smart to become one of the king's brief conquests. She knew how to manipulate a vain-glorious man, and she married him and became queen. Her daughter, Ethelfleda, was packed off to the nunnery at Rum's Eg, and Elfrida bore Edgar a son, Ethelred. Ethelred was not, however, next in line to be king, because Edgar already had a son called Edward.

When he was thirty-three years old, Edgar died, choking on a fishbone whilst trying to scratch his pox scabs. It was now time for Elfrida to ensure that her son become king. She stabbed Edward to death at Corfe Castle in Dorset, whilst pretend-ing to offer him a drink, thus ensuring that Ethelred became king (though he wasn't quite ready). She then built an abbey at Wherwell and settled down very comfortably.

One evening, though, she sat by the crystal-clear waters of the River Test. She'd had a few drinks, and was admiring her reflection in the water – for she had never lost her beauty, not least because the waters of the Test were always known as being good for the complexion. As she gazed at her own reflection, she saw a terrible reflection loom behind hers. It was a terrifying creature with the head of a cockerel and the body of a dragon – and the shock was so great that she tumbled into the river and drowned.

It is said that the name Wherwell derives from Whore's Well, and that the whore in question is Elfrida – because if a woman puts it about a bit she is called a whore, whereas if a man does so he can be called Edgar the Peaceful. Anyway, my dictionary of place names says that Wherwell means 'bubbling streams', and I'm sure the author has done his research in a proper, academic manner, rather than just listened to a lot of old stories, so I guess he knows. As for that creature that gave Elfrida such a shock, well, that must have been the Wherwell Cockatrice, and this leads us to the next story.

THE WHERWELL COCKATRICE

A hen laid her first egg. Oh – she was so proud – she clucked and chuckled, she puffed out her feathers and paraded round the yard, whilst the old, experienced hens watched her with bemusement. The River Test bubbled and rippled nearby, the bell from the abbey tolled across the water meadows, and the singing of the nuns drifted through the summer air.

There is always something to spoil a sylvan scene, though; something dark that comes crawling into the beautiful picture. That which is dark is often formed by misfortune, and in this case an enormous female toad had herself lost her babies – though don't toads always lose their eggs? That is, after they've survived the attentions of a heaving mass of toads, and broken free of the vice-like embrace of the male toad.

This toad, however, watched the hen preening herself in front of the cynical old hens. The toad crept forward and started

to push the egg. She pushed it across the meadow, through damp, toady places by the river, and down into the vaults of Wherwell Abbey. There she squatted, damply, over the egg until it hatched.

When a toad hatches a hen's egg there can be only one result. A cockatrice. Head of a cockerel, body of a dragon. It grew and grew in the darkness, whilst its doting stepmother brought it woodlice and slugs, maggots and worms. Then it ate its stepmother, and continued to grow. Finally, when it was the size of a calf, it crawled up the steps and out into the wide world. The wide Wherwell world. As the sunlight tormented its sensitive skin, screaming nuns ran before it – so it ate one. To escape the hateful sun, it crawled towards the riverbank until it found a damp hole big enough to squat in.

Every so often, always growing, it would crawl forth and eat cattle, and sheep, and goats – and sometimes people, though they weren't very nourishing. In the evening, it took to crawling up a very strong tree, swallowing the occasional passing bird, and watching the world with a baleful eye. Knights from all over Hampshire, and even Berkshire and Sussex, came to slay the cockatrice, but it would just give them a withering look, and a reptilian tongue would dart out from its avian beak, and that would be the end of them.

Finally, a cockatrice slayer arrived from faraway Sussex. He was Egbyrt Green, from Dragon's Green, first cousin to Jim

Pulk the Lyminster dragon slayer, and he had guile as well as guts. He waited till the cockatrice had lowered itself into its damp hole next to the river, and then he crept forward and lowered a polished mirror down the hole. The cockatrice awoke, to find that it was gazing at its own reflection, and, with a terrible squawk, it set about the monster. All night it fought itself, till, battered and exhausted, it lay down, gasping for breath. Then Egbyrt Green climbed down into the hole, and cut off the cockatrice's head. For his work, he was awarded four acres of land in Harewood Forest, and to this day it is known as Green's Copse.

Now, some people have said that the cockatrice was hatched from a duck's egg, but they really need to look at their biology books. If the cockatrice had emerged from a duck's egg it would have had the head of a drake – this story was probably invented to explain the peculiar aversion Wherwell people used to have for duck eggs. The cockatrice was immortalised in a peculiar weathervane that was placed upon the church in the days when people accepted the presence of grotesques and monstrous weathervanes sharing their worship, because they couldn't afford to take a sentimental view of life. In later times, the weathervane was deemed unsuitable for a place of worship, taken down, and put on a barn. It has since found its way to Andover Museum, and, if you don't believe my story, you can go there and see for yourself!

THE RAREY BIRD

I did hear another version of the Wherwell Cockatrice story. I'd been telling stories in Andover shopping centre, and afterwards I went for a pint. A man who had heard me tell stories leaned on the bar next to me. He told me that he came from Wherwell, but had lived in Andover for years now, because country people can't afford to live in the country any more. He was pulling my leg with the story, but I liked it.

He said that the cockatrice wasn't aggressive at all, it was friendly and affectionate. The only problem was that it didn't stop growing. As it was so unique, indeed rare, people called it the Rarey Bird. It grew and grew and the good nuns of Wherwell Abbey kept feeding it, but finally they knew it was going to eat them all out of house and home; the only thing left to do was to dispose of it. So they took it down to one of the Test Valley quarries, and, with tree trunks as levers, prepared to lever it over the edge of a cliff. As they did so, it turned round and gazed at the nuns in an admonishing way, and, with a tear rolling down its beak, it started to sing: 'It's a long way to tip a Rarey.'

The Detectorist's Story

Andover is a strange town. In 1949, Brian Vesey-Fitzgerald wrote that:

Andover is not a beautiful place. It is modern. I have no objection to modernity, but in parts of Andover the present-day builder has been given a free hand and the result is just hideous … I have no doubt that the result of his labours will shortly fall down.

Perhaps the results of these labours have fallen down, but the buildings erected in the 1980s are not much better. Yet some of these estates border right onto the country, and it's possible to step straight out into beautiful Hampshire countryside, an area stuffed full of archaeology; so much so that Andover has its own specialist museum of the Iron Age.

Andover also has some very odd things, like a massive army surplus store, where you don't just buy articles of clothing, you can buy old jeeps. One time, I was wandering through it when I came across a bloke I'd met before, when I'd been telling stories for bikers' children at a motorcycle rally. I'm always a little suspicious of blokes who wear military gear, but who aren't in the army; however, we got talking. He lived an interesting life, one that tended to be somewhat on the periphery of the law. It was a country sort of a life, but, if he went trout fishing in the Test, he wasn't the sort of man to trouble himself with a permit, and if he went shooting pheasants, he probably wouldn't be asking the landowner's permission. He was also a metal-detectorist. I rather imagine that he was the sort of detectorist who would drive archaeologists mad – cutting clumsily through archaeological sites for 'treasure', and never handing any findings over to the landowner or the state. Anyway, knowing my love of stories, and possibly wanting to show me that 'I didn't really know nothing', he told me a story. It fitted with much that I knew about the Test Valley, and it fits in here.

He was detectoring on a hill by the Test Valley – I don't know which hill, he wasn't saying, so it could have been anywhere between Michelmersh and Longparish. The Test Valley is full of archaeological finds and stories of treasure. At the top of the hill, the detectorist came across an old ruined cottage – nothing really left of it except the oblong shape of the footings, all covered in moss and lichen, and surrounded by elder bushes. It was a warm day, but when the detectorist stepped into the oblong, everything went freezing cold, and he stepped out again in alarm. As he did so, he heard the signal through the headphones, so he put the detector down and stepped back into the oblong with the spade.

'What the hell do you think you're doing?' said the farmer, clutching a shotgun.

'Sorry mate,' said the detectorist, 'I hope I'm not trespassing.' Of course, he knew he was trespassing, but it's unwise to pick an argument with a man clutching a twelve bore, and if you're not too antagonistic then the worse that can happen is that you're asked to leave. The farmer escorted him down the hill and warned him not to come back, but he also said a strange thing, 'It's not for my benefit I don't want you digging up there; it's for your benefit – lowlife though you may be. It's a bad place.'

'Does he seriously think he'll frighten me away?' thought the detectorist – like scaring a child with a ghost story – and yet it was a strange place. Anyway, the detectorist had to walk down the road to his white van, and drive back to Andover. The metal-detector had signalled, though – so he was going to return. He returned on a night of the full moon (which is not the best time to go creeping about the countryside) but it was also a very cloudy night.

As he walked up the hill, he felt a real foreboding, and, tough guy though he thought he was, he was tempted to head back to the van. He carried on to the top, though, and, as he approached the oblong shape of the old cottage, a black cloud drifted in front of the face of the moon and everything went pitch dark. He stepped into the stone oblong and was immediately over-whelmed by fear; it was like being crushed by one of those dreams where you know you're dreaming but you can't wake up. He was crouched at one end of the oblong, his face con-

torted with terror, and there was something terrible, darker than the darkness itself, at the other end of the oblong – and it was squelching, sliding, slithering towards him.

Just then, the cloud cleared away from the moon, and everything lit up. Then there were voices, and the beams of torches, and there was the farmer with two policemen. Well, the detectorist hadn't got anything, and he'd caused no damage, but the police knew him, and were happy to bang him up for the night in Andover police station. This, then, is nearly the end of the story.

'There is just a bit more,' the detectorist told me, 'and I've not told anyone this before, because I know they'd take the piss – but you're a storyteller so you might know what I'm talking about.' And this is what he said:

I was up there, crouched in that oblong, with something bad coming at me. Well, before the cloud cleared away from the moon and the bloody boys in blue arrived, something else happened. All the fear just slipped away from me. I felt all light and happy inside, and I wasn't on nothing! What had been dark was light: and I seemed to see right through that light into the hill. I'll tell you what, there were people there, but they weren't like us, they were the other people. There was music too, but I didn't hear it with my ears, I heard it more with my mind. Time was different – what might be a hundred years in our time was just a minute in theirs. I was going to step into that light, and do you know what, if I had done so I reckon I would never have been seen again, but it was then that the farmer turned up with the boys in blue. I'm glad he did, but I still wonder what would have happened if I had stepped into the hill.

What if …?

That was the story that the detectorist told me, and I thought to myself, 'This is a folk tale; it's the hollow hills again, the Kingdom under the Hill.' The Test Valley is full of fragments of treasure legend: the horse with golden shoes buried under Money Bunt Wood, near Longstock; the treasure buried in a bank of earth by the fool who thought that was what was meant by putting your money in the bank; the treasure under Wherwell Abbey, with the body of a man entombed with it … and these stories are still growing – there is now the story of the metal-detectorist on the hill.

If I could credit this man, and so properly attribute the story, I would. This is one reason why I'd like to find him again. The other reason is that he flogged me his white van, and two weeks later it seized up on the M3. I reckon he stitched me up.

Eight

THE FAR NORTH

In Derbyshire, the village of Eyam is well known for its plague story: how the plague struck the unfortunate village, and the rector organised the villagers to selflessly quarantine themselves until the plague had run its course. Most of the villagers died, but they kept the terrible infection from spreading. Hampshire has a similar story – but the horror is greater, because the humanity it shows is all too flawed, as it usually is.

CHUTE'S BROADWAY

If we go north of Andover, we come to some really wild countryside: the high, windblown border between Hampshire and Wiltshire. We also come to Chute's Broadway. Chute's Broadway is part of an old Roman Road, but it isn't straight! It skirts the hill above a crescent-shaped dry valley, and, for once, the Romans allowed the road to follow the topography. Down in the valleys the whole area is a maze of country lanes, though it's possible to spot the villages from the high downs. It is not so easy to spot Vernham Dean, however, because it sits in a hollow in the hills, and when the trees are in leaf it disappears altogether.

It was bad luck for the village to be hit by the plague; maybe someone from the pox-ridden Great Wen of London had passed through. The rector said they must all go up to Haydown Hill, up on the fresh and airy heights of the downs, by that ancient old road, Chute's Broadway. The rector then undertook to bring food and drink up to the strange camp of trauma-tised villagers. The community built themselves rough huts, and waited for provisions, huddled together, as the wind blew across the high downs.

The rector fully intended to return – he was a humane man and he loved his parishioners – but his nerve failed him; the thought of those terrible buboes growing in the damp places of his body appalled him. He couldn't bring himself to ascend that hill with food and drink, and remained, cowering, in the village, hoping he could sustain the villagers with his prayers. Up on the hill, up by the lonely sweep of Chute's Broadway, the villagers perished of thirst, hunger, and plague. The plague had already infected the rector, though, and so he himself perished, away from his flock.

Now, should you go walking on Chute's Broadway by the light of a full moon, you might see the rector of Vernham Dean toiling up the hill with sacks of provisions and contain-ers of water – but, like poor Sisyphus, he can never reach the top.

The memory of plague continues to haunt Chute's Broadway. Another story tells that a man – and maybe it was the man who brought the plague to Vernham Dean – had lost his family to the infection, and he fled into the countryside to live like wild old Merlin, or King Orpheus, torn apart with grief and pain. One night, he was sleeping in a copse, when

he was awoken by music. When he peered out from between the branches, he saw, advancing along Chute's Broadway, a whole host of shades and spectres, playing flutes and drums, and all of them swirling and whirling around a black carriage pulled by black horses. At every step of the horses, the crowd of spectres seemed to increase.

The terrified man seized a stick from his smouldering fire, but, as the multitude drew closer, the stick grew two legs, extended two arms, and the glowing end became two fiery eyes. The stick leaped from the man's hand and started to dance around the fire. The man seized his axe and tried to swipe at it, but the axe grew long black hair and joined the stick in the dancing. As the throng passed, they joined it too.

The man realised that Mistress Plague herself was in the carriage, and, as it proceeded down Chute's Broadway, he saw the trees, the bushes, the owls and the foxes all transform into tall, thin spectres, and dance around the carriage. All the man could do was to thank God he was still alive, and the next morning he turned his face south, and began the long walk to Southampton and a ship to faraway Newfoundland.

The shock of the plague remains strong in the folk tales, and it is little wonder. Hampshire is not so very far from London, and the fear in the county of that foul pox brewing up in the Great Wen must have been strong. There is, indeed, a story from Preston Candover, not far from Basingstoke, that a man who was fleeing London and the plague entered Preston Candover, and there succumbed to the disease. The villagers wouldn't touch him; they shot his horse, and dragged man and horse into a pit, and buried them. His valuables went with him – and so we get another story of buried treasure!

COMBE GIBBET

Those high border-country downs do seem to attract terrible tales, and, much though I'd like to provide a 'happily ever after' story, the countryside thereabouts won't oblige!

On the north-west corner of Hampshire, the Wiltshire border gives way to the Berkshire border, and if you wander along the Test Way (now a long way from the River Test), and over Inkpen Beacon into Berkshire, you will see a strange and unsettling sight – a tall double gibbet, known as Combe Gibbet.

'Your map will tell you that you are in Berkshire, but your heart will tell [you] you're still in Hampshire.' I can do no better than once again quote Brian Vesey-Fitzgerald, because I've come across no one who writes about Hampshire better than he does.

I am standing on Inkpen Beacon, a thousand feet high. And I am not in Hampshire at all, but in Berkshire. And that only goes to show how foolish are the maps. Not so very long ago Inkpen was in Hampshire. Spiritually, geologically, in every way but cartographically it is in Hampshire still: geographically, too (despite what the maps may say), for Inkpen is the natural frontier on the

north. Inkpen belongs to the Hampshire downs and not to the Berkshire downs that are so different from it in every respect. And so to look on those wild hills I stand on the greatest of them. I am in Hampshire. The map lies; not I.

Now, this is the story about how a piece of Hampshire ended up in Berkshire, and it isn't a pleasant story. Combe Gibbet isn't the original gibbet; it has been a tradition that, as one gibbet starts to rot away, or gets struck by lightning, or – as in 1965 and 1969 – gets sawn down in protests against capital punishment, it is replaced. The original gibbet was erected in the seventeenth century.

Once upon a time, in a seventeenth-century sort of a time, there was a widow woman who lived in Combe, and a married man who lived in Inkpen. The widow woman was ample, and warm, and friendly – and a most excellent cook – and they began an affair. How the affair began I don't know, but I know how it ended.

The man grew more and more bitter against his wife; she was far too busy with the hard graft of being the wife of a farm labourer, and with bringing up their children, to spare him much attention. One summer's day, the adulterous couple stole up onto the downs, but these assignations had been noticed by Mad Tom of Walbury. Oh dear me; dribbling with anticipation (for Mad Tom was a peeping Tom), he followed them up the path, and crouched behind a bush. The couple set to with gusto, and Tom watched, sweating profusely. But then Tom saw someone else come up the track, and, oh dear me, it was the man's wife. Tom's eyes goggled at the thought of another kind of encounter. The wife saw the couple and let out a terrible cry. Oh dear God – the man leapt up and seized his wife, and pushed her face into a hornets' nest, with the widow woman screaming and clawing at him, and trying to drag him away. But he held his poor wife till she was dead, and the widow was nearly mad with horror; then he took the body to a dew pond and threw it in. Ever since then, the pond has been known as Murderer's Pool.

But Mad Tom was back down in the village, and he was screaming and gibbering, 'Murder – murder – oh dear God – murder!' and the villagers ascended the hill and found the couple, and found the body floating face-down in the dew pond.

The villagers sent to Winchester for a justice, so that a proper trial could take place. In Winchester, though, the wild hills of Combe and Inkpen were far away and useless. To the Winchester authorities, it was an area more foreign than London Town, and they weren't interested. So the people appealed to the authorities in Berkshire, and Newbury is a lot closer to Inkpen Beacon than Winchester. So the Berkshire authorities arrived and erected a double gibbet, and hanged the man from one side and the woman from the other. This, plus the trial, put them to some expense, and so they claimed Combe and Inkpen Beacon as payment.

Now, the real reason for the boundary change (which came a lot later than the seventeenth century), may have been about roads and accessibility, but stories, as they travel through time, absorb information like sponges. This story is based in historical fact, but I haven't, for instance, found any mention of Mad Tom in any versions of the story preceding 1949 – though I'm prepared to be put right on this. In 1948, one Alan Cooke, along with a chap called John Schlesinger, made a film called *Black Legend*. Schlesinger was still a university student, but he went on to become a famous director – *Midnight Cowboy* and *Marathon Man* are two of his films. *Black Legend* was based on the Combe Gibbet story, and there was a character called Mad Tom, played by a young Robert Hardy. *Black Legend* was first shown in the Village Hall, Inkpen, on 10 June 1949, and if Mad Tom entered the oral tradition that evening, it only goes to show that folk tales are always developing.

There is more to the story, though. Tarred and wrapped in chains, the bodies swung back and forth as the winds blew across the wild downs. Finally, the skeletons and the chains fell to the ground in pieces. Shortly after this, a local farmer found trouble: his sheep took ill and wouldn't feed, and began to die. He tried everything to cure them, but to no avail. One day, however, he came across pieces of the chains in Murderer's Pool. So the chains were buried, and the rector of St Michael's Church in Inkpen came up, and so did the rector of St Swithun's Church in Combe. The two rectors said words over the buried chains, and the farmer's sheep grew fat again. But St Swithun wept, and the reason he wept was human folly, carelessness and violence – not because Newbury had purloined a little piece of Hampshire from Winchester!

The Devil's Highway

A mate of mine is a tarmac doctor – that is, he has a doctorate in tarmacology. He is an expert on road surfaces, and nothing pleases him more than sitting in the pub looking at moving images of the heat transference between road surfaces and vehicle tyres on his laptop. One evening, he told me that the next day he had to go back to the Devil's Highway. I was intrigued; did he mean the M3 or the M27?

'Motorways are the safest roads,' he told me – no, he just meant a very minor road called Park Lane on the border between Hampshire and Berkshire. It was just that, regardless of how the road was surfaced, it always seemed to end up with potholes, and there seemed to be no logical, geological or engineering reason for this. And the men working on the road didn't like it; they called it the Devil's Highway. I didn't particularly expect to hear of superstition from road workers in hi-viz jackets, but there were some very odd stories of men becoming somehow possessed and marching off down the road.

'Possessed by what?'

'Roman soldiers.' Ah.

For Park Lane is near Silchester, the site of the important old Roman city of Calleva Atrebatum, where the Roman road from Londinium forked off in different directions: one to Clavsentvm (now Bitterne Manor in Southampton) and one to Durnovaria (now Dorchester). Park Lane follows the boundary between Hampshire and Berkshire, and I later discovered that the Roman highway from London

to Silchester was known as the Devil's Highway. There was a legend that travellers on the road could be seized by the spirits of those old marching Roman soldiers, and find themselves marching down the road at an unforgiving pace, looking straight ahead, unable to stop even though they were exhausted and their feet were bleeding; so this story was still alive. The picture of a man in a hi-viz jacket, marching down the road like a Roman soldier, seemed rather comical to me, though I'm sure it wouldn't seem comical if you were that man.

There are, though, stories in this part of Hampshire that lose the macabre nature of those stories from the high downs, and start to become really rather silly.

Onion and the Imp

Once upon a time in Silchester, Calleva Atrebatum, there was a giant, and his name was Onion. He wasn't the brightest of giants, though it has to be said that giants are not generally known for their intellectual powers. Not far away, on the border between Hampshire and Berkshire, there lived an imp, and he was irritating, as imps tend to be. His greatest pleasure in life was to tease the giant Onion by shouting rude things at him, such as 'onion bum' and 'garlic brain' and 'shallot shanks', and then watch the giant leap around in a helpless rage. One day, however, the imp went too far, and shouted, 'Pickled onion brain – beetroot bum.' The enraged giant scooped up a stone and hurled it at the imp; it landed on top of the imp and flattened him. That was the end of the imp and it serves him right. Ever since then, there has been a stone next to the Silchester Road, where Hampshire meets Berkshire, and it is called the Imp Stone. If you look at it carefully, you will see the imprints of the giant Onion's fingers.

The rotting city of Calleva Atrebatum must have been a strange sight to Saxon eyes: a city from a past that was more technologically advanced than their present, just mouldering away. Stories attached themselves to it; it was said that Arthur was crowned king there. Camden, in 1610, writes that by then it was surrounded by great oak trees, and that to enter within you had to stoop through an old postern called Onion's Hole, and that you could dig up Roman coins; folk called them Onion's pennies. But let's leave Silchester, Calleva Atrebatum, and wander down the road to Tadley God Help Us.

TADLEY GOD HELP US

Tadley God Help Us is a village (a small town really) in Hampshire. The story to explain the 'God help us' appellation is that at the end of the nineteenth century, or maybe the beginning of the twentieth, a balloonist descended on Tadley. The balloonist walked up to a cottage door and asked where he was. The terrified cottager, seeing that the oddly dressed stranger had descended from the heavens, dropped to his knees and exclaimed, 'Oh Lord almighty, this is God-forsaken Tadley, God help us.' Since then, smart and sophisticated people who fly in the skies have called the place Tadley God Help Us.

Now, Tadley is out on heathland, and in a rural area, but it was never *that* remote. I rather agree with Vesey-Fitzgerald when he places the story in Tangley, a remote village set in a narrow chalk cleft up in the downs near Chute's Broadway. However, the story has attached itself to Tadley, and that may be because of the storytelling proclivities of the Tadley broomsquires.

Tadley isn't a particularly prepossessing place – though I love going there to tell stories in the excellent library, may God pre-

serve it. If you look at the house next to Tadley Library, a
perfectly ordinary semi-detached, you may notice that there
are besoms (broomsticks) leaning against the wall in the
porch, and then you may notice a plaque on the wall. The
plaque shows that here dwells the officially approved sup-
plier of besoms and pea sticks to Her Majesty the Queen. The
heathland around Tadley was full of birch coppices (providing the brush for besoms) and hazel (providing the handles),
and Tadley was a major centre for besom production. Arthur
Nash made besoms here, and I bought one — not for any
witchy 'new-agey' nonsense, but as a practical tool, to clear
up leaves and sweep the yard. Sadly, Arthur Nash has now
passed on, but I believe that his wife and son still continue
the tradition, even making besoms for the Harry Potter films
— though I imagine it is hard, now, trying to sustain a business
making quality handmade implements.

At one time, though, when Tadley was full of besom makers,
these experts, known as broomsquires, were great raconteurs
and storytellers, and they probably enjoyed spreading the Tadley
God Help Us stories. Like many a village in England, there
are stories of treacle mines and bacon ghosts, but here is one I
heard. I was telling stories at a country fair, and a broomsquire,
who had heard it from one of the old Tadley originals back in
the early sixties, told the following story to me:

THE MAN IN THE MOON AND THE BROOMSQUIRE

A broomsquire had been peddling his besoms out to the east of Tadley, and on his way home he stopped for a drink or three at Hall in the Hole, now long gone. Night fell, and he still had to traverse Pamber Forest to get himself back to civilisation and Tadley. As he stumbled through the forest, he came across an open clearing that he didn't recognise – and across it there was a line of white stones, all shining under the light of the full moon. He followed the stones, but, as he did so, his feet started to sink into the ground – and this was strange in the dry heathland. So he stepped up onto the stones, and stepped from one to another like they were stepping stones. Then, oh dear me, a cloud drifted in front of the moon, and it must have been a big, black, thunder cloud, because he couldn't see his hand in front of his face. He stopped, balanced on a stone, but then he felt it begin to sink. Oh Lord, the glutinous, soggy ground was up to his ankles, then it was up to his knees. When the boggy substance reached his thighs, the cloud cleared from the moon and the broomsquire realised he was up to his arse in treacle; he had stumbled into the Tadley treacle mine. Just then, a magpie alighted on a stone.

'Trrrk Trrrk Trrrk,' said the magpie.

One for sorrow…

'That's all I need,' thought the broomsquire, 'to be watched by a bad omen as I sink into a treacle mine.'

'What are you doing?' said the magpie. Now, this was surprising.

'I be standing on a stone in a treacle mine, and the treacle is up to my waist,' replied the unfortunate broomsquire.

'Why?' enquired the bird.

'I don't know.'

'If you don't know why, I won't. Why don't you fly away?'

'I can't. People can't fly.'

'Bloody fools,' said the bird.

The broomsquire tried to remain polite. 'I be standing on a stone in a treacle mine, and the water's up to my chest,' he said, 'could you help me please?'

'Don't know about that,' said the magpie, eyeing the broom-squire over its beak in a supercilious manner.

'Please – I be standing on a stone in a treacle mine, and the water be up to my neck.'

'Oh, very well,' said the magpie, 'Allow me to introduce my wife.'

'Trrrk Trrrk Trrrk,' said Mrs Magpie.

Two for joy…

'Reach out for our feet,' said the magpie. The broomsquire grasped their feet and they flapped and they flapped, and they hauled him out of the treacle mine, and way up into the air above Pamber Forest.

'Thank 'ee, thank 'ee,' cried the broomsquire, 'will you be setting me down in Tadley now?'

'No,' said the magpie.

'No?'

'No – because I don't like you. You and your kind throw stones at us when you're gathering your blessed birch sticks. You chase us away, you shoot at us, and you hang us upside down from fences. I don't like you.'

'Please – I'll never throw another stone,' pleaded the broom-squire. But the pair of magpies had taken him high into the sky, and, when they reached some shining, white ground, they threw him down. Then off they flew, shouting rude things at him, and calling out, 'Trrrk Trrrk Trrrk.' The broomsquire dragged himself to his feet, and looked around. Where was he? He was on the moon.

The poor broomsquire sat on the rim of a crater and began to cry. 'I only wanted a few drinks. I only want to get home. I'm just a humble broomsquire – what did I do to deserve this? Boo hoo hoo.'

Just then, a little man with a very long beard and a pointy hat popped his head out of the crater.

'Who are you?' said the little man.

'Who are you?' said the broomsquire.

'I asked first,' said the little man.

'I'm a broomsquire from Tadley.'

Well, b✱✱✱✱✱ off back to Tadley, then.'

'I can't, I'm on the moon – and who are you?'

'Who do you think I am? I'm the man in the moon, and I don't want *you* on the moon.'

'And I don't want to *be* on the moon!' wailed the broomsquire.

So the man in the moon picked up a besom – a proper moon-made besom – and he swept the broomsquire up into the sky. The broomsquire found himself falling and falling, into the world.

'Oh dear Lord,' he thought, 'I'm going to be splattered.'

Just then a goose flew by, folded its wings, and started to plummet downwards with him.

'Honk,' said the goose.

'Aaaaargh!' said the broomsquire.

'What are you doing?' asked the goose.

'Falling to my death,' said the broomsquire.

'Hold on to my feet then,' said the goose.

'Now, this has happened before,' thought the broomsquire – but a drowning man will clutch at a straw, and a plummeting man will clutch at a goose's feet, so he grasped them. The goose spread its wings, levelled off, and flew southwards.

'Climb up onto my back,' said the goose, and so the broomsquire climbed onto its back and, as if he was astride a flying horse, found himself flying over Hampshire. There, in the moonlight, were towns and hamlets, churches and barns, forests

and copses, roads and rivers, field and farms – and then there
was the sea and the whole coast from Sussex to Dorset, and the
Isle of Wight ahead of them.

'You're not dropping me off at Tadley, then?' enquired the
broomsquire.

'I'm going to France,' said the goose, 'and you're a very fat
broomsquire and I can't support you much longer; you'll have
to get off.'

'I CAN'T!' screamed the broomsquire, 'I'LL BE KILLED!'

'There, there,' said the goose in a patronising tone, and
swooped down, low over the sea.
'See that ship? If it's not sailing to Southampton, it's sailing for
Pompey. You just drop into the sea, shout for help, and they'll
fish you out.'

So, when he thought that the goose was nearest the sea, the
broomsquire dropped off its back, tumbled into the sea, and sank
like a stone. And along came a whale and swallowed him all up.
It was disgusting in the whale's belly – all sorts of flotsam and
jetsam floating about, besides dead fish and all sorts of rotting,
smelly things. A voice boomed out, all muffled and strange, and
the broomsquire couldn't make out the words.

'Beg pardon?' he called, being a polite sort of a chap.

'TICKLE MY TONSILS,' boomed the voice of the whale,
and the broomsquire did. The whale was violently sick and
threw the broomsquire up onto a little shingle beach. And there

he was, all wet and bedraggled, and covered in whale vomit, on Spice Island in old Portsmouth. He had a long walk home.

Ever since then, though, it was said that his besoms had a bit of magic moon dust about them, and the sort of people who bought them didn't use them for practical purposes, but danced around them naked, and stuff like that. Speaking personally, I'll stick to the practical usages – because if you should ever see, as I have done, a leaf-clearing contest between two gardeners, and one has a besom, and the other has one of those noisy, two-stroke leaf blowing machines, you'll know that it's the besom that wins every time.

CRICKET, SINGLE-STICK WRESTLING AND BARE-KNUCKLE BOXING

Hampshire Hogs always had a fondness for battering each other, so the county was known for the violence of its sports. Hambledon, in mid-Hampshire, is well known for being the birthplace of cricket, and, whilst cricket may be thought of as a rather gentlemanly game, anyone who has faced a speeding cricket ball may well think otherwise. (I do think that the Hampshire cricket commentator, John Arlott, who has himself entered folklore, was, however, a true gentleman, and the kind of man desperately missed by modern sport.)

Hampshire was also known for single-stick wrestling, where combatants were armed with sticks. The Reverend J.E. Jackson wrote:

They fought bareheaded, with the left arm fastened to the waist, so that they might not use it to ward off blows. To hit an opponent on the face was against the rules: but to hit him on the top of the head was the grand point, and the grandest point of all was to hit him so as to produce blood.

We've already encountered bare-knuckle boxing in Wickham, but if we are to travel eastwards from Tadley, we come to where Hampshire borders with Surrey, and this is a land of sheer, unadulterated savagery.

The Battle of Farnborough

At Farnborough, we have the place that marks the beginning of international boxing championships. It marks it with the brutality that is probably appropriate to the sport, with a fight that entered the public consciousness in the way that turns real events into folklore. The county border is significant to the story. By 1860, bare-knuckle boxing had been outlawed; so, if the fight was raided by the Hampshire police, everyone could leg it (and if they missed the bridge and a boat, swim it) across the River Blackwater into Surrey. The fight took place on Farnborough heathland, outside what was then a village.

John Heenan was a giant Irish-American, who had developed his fighting prowess as an 'enforcer' in the rigged elections of San Francisco. Tom Sayers was only 5ft 8in, but he was driven by his background from the slums of Brighton and London. He was hard as nails, and boxing was, as it always has been, a way to earn fame and money, and a way to escape.

Vast crowds of people descended from London Town, and these crowds included notables like the Prince of Wales, Charles Dickens, W.M. Thackeray, and – so it is said – Lord Palmerston, the prime minister himself. Plainly the rich, the famous, and the high ranking could be turned on by the sight of working-class men battering each other to a pulp.

The fight was long and savage. At first, Heenan knocked Sayers round the ring, and it looked like no contest; but then Sayers started to move, and he inflicted so much damage on Heenan that the prize-fighter was temporarily blinded. The contemporary descriptions, and the local folklore, describe how Sayers would inflict damage, and then stand back and examine Heenan, generously letting the man recover. This seems highly unlikely; in England, we like to portray our heroes as gentlemanly underdogs, and make up stories to fit this image!

The fight went on for forty rounds, after which Heenan was unable to see, and Sayers was fighting with a broken arm. Finally, Heenan forced Sayers' neck onto the ropes, and held him there till his face turned black, his tongue protruded from his mouth, and his eyes were popping from their sockets. At this point, the highly partial crowd stormed the ring and cut the rope; and, in the ensuing disorder, the police were forced to act. In they charged and there followed utter chaos – crowd battling police, general brawling, and folks legging it across the county border to Surrey. The fight was declared a draw, and, after this, the 9th Marquess of Queensberry came up with the 'Queensberry Rules', to ensure fairer fighting. The Battle of Farnborough is often taken as being the world's first title fight.

A Highwayman's Heath

In Victorian times, north-east Hampshire was urbanising rapidly. Mrs Juliana Horatia Ewing, a lover of folklore and writer of children's fairy tales, wrote about Aldershot:

Take a Highwayman's Heath. Destroy every vestige of life with fire and axe … then shall the winds come, from the east and from the west, from the north and from the south, and shall raise on your shaven heath clouds of sand that would not disgrace a desert in the heart of Africa.

On that shaven heath has grown the urban conglomeration of Aldershot, Farnborough, Farnham, Fleet and Camberley. As

heathland, though, it was a dangerous place on the high road
to London. It was said that Dick Turpin haunted this heath, but
the name of Turpin seems to get attached to highwaymen in
general – rather in the way that the name of Arthur is attached
to ancient kings and chieftains. There was, however, only one
Claude Duval.

Duval was a Frenchman who had come to England to
work as a footman for the Duke of Richmond. Monsieur
Duval, however, took up the profession of gentlemanly
highwayman. One fine day, he held up a coach on
Farnborough Heath, but told the gentleman and his wife
that he would only take part of the loot if the gentleman's
wife would dance with him. So, they danced by the roadside while a manservant played the flute. William Pope used
this tale for a poem, and William Powell Frith used it for a
painting.

There was also William Davies, aka the Golden Farmer. He
would also behave in a most gentlemanly manner, so as to show
his victims that he was no mere footpad or cutpurse. He sometimes worked in league with 'Old Mobb' from Romsey, who
rather liked to dress as a woman. The Jolly Farmer Roundabout
on the A30 at Bagshot, just across the border in Surrey, gets its
name from William Davies.

These highwaymen did rather fancy themselves, and there
has always been great snobbery amongst thieves. In 2002, the
newspapers were able to add to these legends, with headlines
such as 'Highwaymen hold up a Stagecoach', when two thugs
held up the Aldershot to Camberley Stagecoach South mini-
bus. They tied up the driver, stole his money as well as the
takings, and drove the bus back to Aldershot. I tend to think
that this sums up highwaymen in general; the robbery would
have been a miserable and traumatic experience for the bus
driver, and so robberies must have been for victims of those
historical highwaymen.

Duval and Old Mobb ended their lives dangling on a rope at Tyburn. Davies ended his on a rope at Salisbury Court, also in London. Salisbury Court was the place where Davies had murdered a butcher, and his life ended at the scene of the crime.

The Treasure of the Basingstoke Canal

So, now most of north-east Hampshire is an urban 'splurge'. Yet there is always hidden magic, and beneath motorways and link roads, in between housing estates and industrial estates, there really is beauty and wildlife – for there is the Blackwater Valley nature reserve. The length of the River Blackwater is a Site of Special Scientific Interest, and a haven for wildlife. There is also the old Basingstoke Canal, which was built to link Basingstoke with London, and a story.

When the canal was being dug at the end of the eighteenth century, some of the 'navvies' (a word to describe the canal construction workers that was taken from the word 'navigate') unearthed a hoard of buried treasure: gold and silver, and the armour of an ancient chieftain. The navvies promptly downed tools and disappeared. They were gone for seven years – in stories, if it's not threes, it's sevens – and when they finally reappeared they were dressed as fine gentlemen. It was said that one of them, who came from the County Cavan in Ireland, became Lord of Farnham, but I can't vouch for the historical authenticity of that.

The Blackwaterbeat

Folklore and folk stories – always developing. So we come to 1961, The Beatles, and Aldershot. As I took a drink in an

Aldershot social club, I was told that if it hadn't been for a little mistake, the genre of music known as the Merseybeat might have been called the Blackwaterbeat, which alliterates rather nicely, and the Liverpool sound might have been the Aldershot sound.

In December 1961, The Beatles were booked to play the Palais Ballroom, Aldershot. The story of battling in this part of Hampshire doesn't just refer to bare-knuckle boxing, for this was a north versus south battle, a battle of the bands. The Beatles, from the north, were pitched against Ivor Jay & the Jaywalkers, from the south. Sam Leach, The Beatles' manager, wanted this to be the band's debut in the south.

Unfortunately, there was a communication breakdown with the local newspaper, and the gig wasn't advertised; so only four people turned up as audience. The five-bob fee was quickly dropped, and free entry offered; so finally The Beatles went on in front of an audience of eighteen. This event signalled the end of the career of Leach as The Beatles' manager, and the beginning of Epstein's managership.

It is said that an Aldershot resident complained about the noise; not just the noise of the music, but the noise of The Beatles playing football with bingo balls. This meant that when the Fab Four left the hall at 1 a.m., the Aldershot police ordered them to leave town and to never darken Aldershot's doors again. I don't believe this for a minute, but it makes a good conclusion to the story!

Nine

The Isle of Wight

The Isle of Wight is different. There have been times when I've been booked to tell stories in a school in Cowes, and I've driven the short distance down to the ferry terminal in Southampton, then the short distance to the school, and the temperature gauge in the car hasn't had time to reach its normal level. Yet I have left the mainland and am in another place. It feels different, the light is different and life is a little bit slower. I should certainly have gone by bike!

The stories are different too, though they do connect to stories just across the Solent. There are stories of saints sailing in on millstones and miracles at holy wells; often stories that are more similar to Cornish or Breton stories, than mainland Hampshire ones.

Cork Heads

Islanders are known as Cork Heads. Those searching for some sort of pretentious superiority will say, 'No, they are

called "caulk heads", and they are called this because of a
past industry in Carisbrooke, where people caulked up boats,
which is sealing up the planking with oakum.' This is nonsense. They are called Cork Heads because they have corky
heads. Most of the Island nowadays is occupied by 'over-
landers', or 'overners' – people from the mainland; usually,
it would seem, from London, Lancashire and Yorkshire, and
we can't blame those people for wanting to escape. Cork
Heads, however, are those who can claim to have generations
of Islanders behind them. If there is a boat out at sea, and
on board that boat there are Cork Heads and overners, and
along comes a terrible storm, and the boat is sunk – well, the
overners will plummet down to Davy Jones' Locker, but the
Cork Heads will remain on the surface, bobbing about with
their corky heads until the lifeboat comes along and pulls
them out.

How the Island got its Name

In Hampshire and East Dorset, the Isle of Wight is simply
known as 'the Island', occasionally being called 'the Isle of
Widget', with the same sort of humour that gives us 'Cork
Head'. The Romans called it Vectis; the name 'Wight' comes
from the Jutes.

In 534, Cerdic and his son Cynric conquered the island, and
Cerdic gave it to his nephews, Stuf and Whitgar. It was actually
Stuf who ruled the island, but they thought that the Isle of Stuf
didn't sound too good, so they named it after Whitgar. That's
my theory, and I'm sticking to it.

THE STORY OF ST ARWALD

The last Jutish king of the Isle of Wight was Arwald, and
he's now a saint. The Island remained pagan after most of
the mainland converted to Christianity, and this story con-
cerns the enforced conversion of the Island to Christianity.
I wonder, though, if what was really taking place was a change
from Celtic Christianity to Roman Christianity after the Synod
of Whitby.

King Caedwalla was an Anglo-Saxon king in Wessex, and
he invaded the Isle of Wight with such ruthless slaughter that
it has been suggested that a deliberate policy of ethnic cleans-
ing was being carried out against the Jutes. King Arwald of
Wight was killed in the battle, but his two younger brothers escaped across the water to Ytene, later to be called the
New Forest. They hid deep in the forest – maybe even at
Canterton Glen – but the dark, suspicious inhabitants of
Ytene were from a time before the Jutes. Jutes and Saxons – it
was all the same to them.

So, for gold, Arwald's brothers were betrayed to Caedwalla
and taken to Stoneham, just north of Southampton.
At Stoneham they were put to the sword, but not before they
had been converted to Roman Christianity. Their names were
lost, but collectively the church remembered them as St Arwald.
It seems a strange way to get a sainthood.

And what of that other saint, St Wilfrid, who we heard about
converting the Meon Valley? Caedwalla gave him a quarter of
the Island. A fine pair of warlords, those two.

STORIES OF ST BONIFACE

Boniface was another saint. He was born in Devon, but joined
the monastery at Nutscelle, which was somewhere on the

River Itchen, north of Southampton. His eyes were fixed on missionary work in Germany, so he thought he would get a bit of practice by going to the Isle of Wight.

He climbed onto a millstone, and sailed down the River Itchen and out into Southampton Water, the great channel that connects Southampton to the Solent. The millstone then traversed the Solent, sailed round the Island, and pitched Boniface ashore at what is now called Bonchurch, a name that means Boniface's Church. He climbed to a vantage point, now called the Pulpit Rock, and preached to the fishermen. They converted forthwith.

The Finite Mind

Even a great saint could have doubts about his faith, though. One day, Boniface was walking the shoreline, tormented by doubts, and praying for a sign. There was no clap of thunder, no bolt of lightning; instead, he saw, ahead of him, a little boy digging a hole in the sand. As Boniface watched, the boy took a shell to the sea, filled it with water, and poured the water into the hole – whereupon it sank into the sand. The boy repeated the operation several times, and then threw a tantrum! He hurled the shell at the ground and burst into angry, frustrated tears.

'Why are you crying, little cork head?' asked the kindly Boniface.

'I wanted to empty the sea into the hole, but I can't, I can't, I can't!' howled the boy.

Boniface was enlightened. 'My mind is finite. How can I fit the infinite into that which is finite?' and his faith was confirmed. This could also explain why it is so difficult to comprehend quantum theory.

Bonny's Well

Behind Bonchurch there is a steep hill, and on the top is

Boniface Down. It is a feature of downs that they are always up; you never go down to a down. On the slope of the hill, somewhere, is a well, known as St Boniface's Well – or, more popularly, Bonny's Well. This was discovered by a lost bishop, with the aid of the saint.

One winter's night, a bishop was riding across Boniface Down, when one of those cold, clammy sea mists came rolling in from the Channel.

The mist from the Channel rose woolly and chill,
And it clung like a pall to the face of the hill,
Blotting out landscape and headland and bay
And through this good Dobbin was picking his way.
While the bishop, a prey to excusable fears.
Could scarce see a fathom in front of his ears —

…wrote Percy G. Stone, a Victorian lover of the Isle of Wight. The bishop then found, to his horror, that his trusty steed, with legs splayed, was slowly sliding down the edge of the hill. Soon they would both be tumbling off a cliff. The horse's downward slide stopped, however, when its hooves entered a damp indentation in the ground. It was Bonny's Well. The bishop immediately dedicated it to St Boniface.

Now, if you can find the well, it will grant you a wish. This will only be possible, however, if you never look behind you as you ascend the 800ft up the down. This is hard, because the climb is strenuous and the view is magnificent. Ships used to lower their topsails as a sign of respect as they passed Bonny's Well, and, on every St Boniface Day, 5 June, the well used to be dressed with flowers. This must always have been a sacred site.

Nowadays it is hard to find the well, but surely this is a good thing? Shouldn't the search be part of the process of a visit to the well, just as the effort to a pilgrimage is as essential as the arrival?

Boniface may, or may not, have really been to the Isle of Wight. It is not at all unlikely; he spent his early adult life in Hampshire. The story of his life, however, seems mainly to be a story of missionary work in Germany, where he is known as Bishop Boniface of Mainz. It may be that Wilfrid studied under Boniface in Germany – which rather suggests that the Isle of Wight Boniface is a figure of legend, possibly carrying older legends, rather than an historical figure. Interestingly, the German legends connect him to pagan symbols and stories; he is said to have chopped down Yggdrasil, the great tree of Thor, and he is sometimes said to be the originator of the Christmas Tree. It would seem that on the Isle of Wight he plays a similar role; he has become attached to pre-Christian traditions. Certainly his stories, like those of St Swithun, are homely and gentle.

THE MYSTERIOUS HERMIT OF THE CRYSTAL WELL

Close to Boniface Down is Ventnor, and close to Ventnor is St Lawrence, which is now a suburb of Ventnor. In *Wayland's Guide: Isle of Wight, Portsmouth and Dockyard*, which dates from approximately 1885, we are told that near the tiny twelfth-century church of St Lawrence (now known as St Lawrence Old Church) there is a crystal well, and in this book I read the strangest fragment of a story. I read that there was a mysterious hermit …

…through whose influence it is said a Pilgrim, in a grey cowl, who had visited the holy land, was assassinated – thus fulfilling the prophesy.

When sainted blood in the burn shall well,
It shall light a flame so hot and snell,
Shall fire the burg from lock to fell
Nor sheeling bide its place to tell,
And Culvert's Nass shall ring its knell.

According to the legend, the prophesy was culminated by the burning of a town, which, it is said, stood on the site now occupied by Woolverton Wood.

This was such a tantalising fragment that I really wanted to know more, and it stuck in my mind for a long time. Then I came across Abraham Elder's 1839 book, *Tales and Legends of the Isle of Wight: With the Adventures of the Author in Search of Them*, and there was the story – and it was another story of the hollow hills. Abraham Elder seems a little roguish, so may well have made it up, but he may also have based his personal rendering of the story on local legend.

Elder tells us that there was a hermit who lived near Culvert's Nass Cliff. He had arrived recently, and was making rather a good living from the local people – selling cures, herbs, and spells. Then things in the area started to go wrong: cattle took ill, the sheep died and the people came to the hermit for help.

'There is a wicked wizard nearby,' whispered the hermit, squinting this way and that when he spoke, 'and he wears a grey cowl. He poisons the wells, and casts evil curses; finish him, and you finish the evil that afflicts us.'

Then, who should come to the crystal well, but a man with a grey cowl, and the villagers cast stones at him; he died with his blood dripping into the well. When they lifted his cowl they found, to their horror, that he was a good old hermit who had lived there many years before, and who had left on a pilgrimage to the holy land.

Their new hermit came by and laughed. The villagers, in their fear and guilt, didn't know what to do, but one villager, Edgar, followed the hermit to Culvert's Nass Cliff, where the hermit struck the ground with his staff. The ground opened up and the hermit descended into the hollow hill, closely followed by Edgar. Inside the hill was a magnificent hall, and there were imps and sprites, and bogles and boggarts – and beautiful little green ladies who insisted that Edgar dance with them. The hermit capered around in the middle of the melee, and Edgar soon saw that he had horns and a pointy tail. Then they all sat down to the feast, at which point Edgar did what he always did before eating: he said grace. There was a bang and a crash, and a smell of brimstone, and Edgar found himself sitting alone on the top of the cliff, with a mist creeping in from the sea, and the sound of the waves on the rocks. When Edgar returned home, there had been a French raid on the village, and Woolverton had been burnt to the ground; not a soul was to be found alive.

It may be that in the *Wayland's Guide* version of the story, the locations have become a little confused. There was a Woolverton Manor at Ventnor, but Woolverton Wood and Culver Cliff are a little further north-east up the coast, in between Sandown and Bembridge. It is interesting that the whole area around the Bembridge Foreland was once a separate island called Bembridge Isle, and the area is still largely separated from the rest of the Isle of Wight by the River Yar. Bembridge Isle has its own saint, the mysterious St Urien – but then, the whole south coast of the Island was once full of saints and hermits.

Wayland's Guide, with its Ventnor location for the story, goes on to tell us that if we walk back to Ventnor from St Lawrence's Church, we might want to look at the Dripping Well: 'it is continually dripping, and in other times

the monks used to come to drink of this water, which is supposed to possess some curative properties.'

Stories ask us to explore – to put our boots on and search.

THE GIANT OF BLACKGANG CHINE

Another hermit on the south coast of the Island got rid of the
giant of Blackgang Chine.

Blackgang Chine is generally known for its amusement park,
and an unfortunate habit of guidebooks to the more pastoral
delights of the Island is to take a rather snobbish swipe at it.
I love the place, and it should not only be part of everyone's
childhood, but also their young parenthood and grandparent-
hood! It was one of the original theme parks, and none the
worse for that: innocent and unsophisticated.

However, should you go past the amusement park, you
would, not so very long ago, have gone down the chine.
A chine is a steep valley, created by a stream that has cut a channel through the soft rock as it flows to the sea; it's a word used
only on the Isle of Wight, and that East Dorset area around
Bournemouth that used to be part of Hampshire. Blackgang
Chine, like most chines, was beautiful – but it could also feel very
desolate. That desolation has now overwhelmed it; it has been
destroyed by a series of landslides, one of which, in 1994, took a
large slab of the amusement park with it.

Once upon a time, Blackgang Chine had two occupants:
a flesh-eating giant and a hermit. (In Abraham Elder's book
there is a poem about this legend, and it is filled with as
many goblins, pixies, floating skulls and dancing skeletons as
Blackgang Chine amusement park; wonderful stuff.) A flesh-
eating giant and a hermit cannot co-exist in the same chine
– especially as the hermit wished to protect people, whilst the
giant gloried in eating them. The brave saint descended the

chine to the giant's lair, and, stamping his staff of mountain ash on the ground, he made the sign of the cross and cursed the giant and all his wicked ways. One of those mists came swirling up the chine and enveloped them both; when it was gone, the valley was desolate and the little stream was blood red. It still was when I wandered down there in the 1990s, but now it's all gone.

Every so often the earth moves, and another piece of land slides into the sea. It is as if the giant is trying to escape from his underground imprisonment.

THE PIED PIPER OF FRANCHEVILLE

Legends that are attached to different places often get transposed to another location; and there are several legends on the Isle of Wight that are also to be found in other places. The Island absorbs stories, so naturally tales are placed there, but any proper Cork Head will tell you that all the stories originated on the Isle of Wight and were pinched by foreigners. Maybe this is the case with the Pied Piper of Francheville. The story is pretty much the same as the Pied Piper of Hamelin, which was popularised by Robert Browning in 1842, but W.H. Auden speculated that the Isle of Wight story really was the original.

Francheville, which means Freetown, is now called Newtown, and should you go there nowadays you won't see many buildings, but you will see a strange sight – a town hall standing all alone. This tells us that the town, on the flat, central north coast of the Island, was once busy and prosperous.

Once upon a time, Francheville was a thriving seaport, with ships at the quayside, a busy marketplace, and streets with names that reflected this mercantile prosperity: Gold Street and Silver Street. But then came the rats. Francheville, with its granaries and food stores, was just right for rats, and this was a real horde of the biggest, meanest, nastiest rats, led by the king of the rats himself. Cats and dogs were brought in to deal with the rat infestation, but they were torn to pieces; where once there was a dog, there was just a pink, wriggling mass of rats' tails and the sound of tearing flesh – horrible – horrible.

The mayor and corporation were desperate for help and so offered a reward of £50 for anyone who could rid the town of the rats. This was the fourteenth century and so £50 was a huge sum of money. And who should arrive at the town? Well, we know, and the reason we know is because we've made a German legend more famous than our own. The piper walked through the town, squeezing the *dudel-sack* of his bagpipes, and his piping was soon accompanied by the squeaking and gibbering of thousands of rats, as they emerged from granaries and hay stacks, shops and kitchens, barns and barrels. This army of rats followed the piper down to the quayside, where he climbed into a rowing boat, and, with the rats swimming behind him, he rowed out to the mud flats. There he resumed his piping whilst the rats clambered onto the mud flats and stuck fast. The piper sat back in the boat and watched as the tide came in and drowned the lot of them. They must have looked a horrible sight when the tide went back out – perhaps that's where the phrase 'you look like a drowned rat' comes from.

Now the mayor started to think what a huge sum of money £50 was, and whether the town could really afford it. If only he'd offered £20; that was still a substantial sum, and surely the piper would have done the job for that. So then the mayor offered the piper £20, and there was an argument. The mayor lost his temper, and said, '£20 it is, take it or leave it.'

Then the piper played a different tune and the children followed him into the woods behind Francheville. When the parents ran after them, they were all gone – vanished into the trees – and the sound of the pipes had faded into the whispering of the wood.

In 1377, the French attacked Francheville – but the generation that would have provided the young fighting men was gone, so only the middle-aged and ancient were there to defend it, and they didn't stand a chance. Francheville was destroyed. Francheville became Newtown, and struggled on, but never regained its former importance. It kept its importance politically though, and the Town Hall was built in the sixteenth century. This was because Newtown had two parliamentary seats; it became one of the most notorious rotten boroughs in England, which lasted till the Reform Act of 1832.

Visitors to the Isle of Wight often neglect this area of the Island's north coast. Naturally enough they go to one of the amusement parks or attractions, or to the lovely undercliff around Ventnor, or to Alum Bay and The Needles. I think that one of the pleasures of the Island, though, is to visit quiet little Newtown and, on a warm summer's evening, watch the red sky over the mud flats, and listen to the sea-birds and waders, and maybe wonder what happened to all those children.

THE BUILDING OF GODSHILL CHURCH

There are several other nationally known legends attached to the Isle of Wight. We have already heard how the Romans were unable to build their capital on Old Winchester Hill because every night the building stones rolled themselves back down into the valley. The same is said of Christchurch Cathedral, which, though it is now in East Dorset, used to be in Hampshire. On the Isle of Wight the story is told about Godshill Church; though, characteristically for the Island, the legend is reversed. The church now stands at the *top* of the hill, and the stories say that the builders were attempting to construct it at the *bottom*. The stones were rolled back up by some super-natural agency – and maybe this made life a bit easier for the labourers, who at least had gravity on their side when rolling them back down. In spite of this, they still had to give up.

One story says that the land at the bottom belonged to a farmer, who was such a sinner that a church could never be built there – something that suited the farmer very well; he didn't want to lose his land. The other story says that the field at the bottom of the hill was a fairy field, and the church would prevent the fairies from holding their revels. So, every night, the fairies toiled up the hill, hauling the stones behind them. Finally, the ecclesiastical authorities had to give up, and, on the day of the church's consecration at the top of the hill, the fairies could be heard holding their revels in the field at the bottom of the hill.

THE PHANTOM PARTY

Another nationally known legend has attached itself to the Isle of Wight, but it has attached itself to a very appropriate place. Knighton Gorges isn't a series of gorges, like Cheddar Gorge or the Avon Gorge; it was once a house, indeed one of the grandest houses on the Island. In 1821, in an appalling fit of pique, it was destroyed by its owner, George Maurice Bisset, because he wanted to prevent his daughter from inher-iting it. This was because she had had the temerity to marry a clergyman without her father's consent. All that is left of the house now are two gateposts standing next to the road under Knighton Down.

In the 1920s, a young man was walking the Island; maybe he was collecting stories. He'd crossed Arreton Down and, as an early winter evening drew in, he knew he needed to find somewhere to sleep for the night. As he ambled down the lane, there were two gateposts with heraldic beasts on the top of them. He was very impressed, and, given that it was New Year's Eve, he wondered if he could get a night's shelter there.

He walked down the drive and saw that there were lights blazing in every window of the manor house, and the sounds of gaiety and laughter; there was a great party going on. It was obviously a fancy-dress party, because the men wore powdered wigs and the women were resplendent in Georgian dresses. He banged on the door, and tapped on the window, but couldn't get any attention. Eventually he gave up; but he was halfway up the drive when he thought he'd go back and try again. As he turned, a black carriage pulled by black horses came thundering towards him from the house; he flung himself into a ditch before he was trampled beneath the hooves. He was shaken, bruised and angry, and decided not to return.

The young man got himself lodgings down in the village. When he told his story to the landlady, she told him that the house was long gone; it had been knocked down in her great-granny's time. The next day, the young man returned and found that there were just two gateposts; there was no drive, no heraldic beasts on the gateposts, and no house. All he could see was a field, a tumbledown barn, an old orchard, and a tangle of weeds.

This is a version of a story found throughout Britain and Ireland, but rarely is the name of the house given so specifically. The Isle of Wight has developed quite a ghost-hunting industry, not least because the Island became a tourist destination in Victorian times. And, should you go on a ghost tour, you will very likely be taken to those gateposts. If you wish to see the house, though, you will have to go alone, and probably on New Year's Eve.

The King's Head

Among its many ghosts, the Island can boast of the head of King Charles I. During the Civil War, the king was imprisoned at Hampton Court, but he escaped to the Isle of Wight. The king had some intention of continuing the war from Carisbrooke Castle, and this put the governor, Colonel Hammond, in a very difficult position. He had little choice but to imprison the king, though at first the king was treated as an honoured guest and allowed the freedom of the Island. The king tried to escape, and so was imprisoned in the castle. Stories arose that, during his escape attempt, he'd taken refuge at Billingham Manor, near Chillerton, but he was unable to stand the claustrophobia of the narrow space he had to hide in, and so returned to Carisbrooke. At Carisbrooke, Colonel Hammond got to hear about another planned escape, and so greeted the king with, 'I have come to take leave of your majesty, for I hear you are going away.' After this, the king was returned to London, where he lost his head on 30 January 1649.

Billingham Manor, however, acquired the king's ghost. In 1928, a couple were renting the manor, and they saw glowing phosphorescence through the cracks around a wooden panel. When they moved the panel, the severed head of Charles I floated in front of them, glowing with a greenish light, till it finally faded into the darkness. It transpired that this apparition was seen every time there was an execution on the Island – and on that very day, in 1928, a prisoner had been executed in Newport. The story may be fanciful, but, to me, the idea that the ghost of an executed king should associate himself with the execution of commoners, is a rather touching aspect of the tale. One of the saddest things, though, is to hear about the death of the king's fourteen-year-old daughter at Carisbrooke in 1650. She had rickets, and she died of pneumonia. Amongst stories of wars and battles, and the manoeuvrings of the mighty, these little vignettes sometimes tell more of reality.

MICHAEL MOREY'S HUMP

To continue the theme of decapitation we come to Michael Morey's Hump, and a man who would murder his own grandson. Michael Morey was a woodsman, and he'd never seen large amounts of money – but the boy had inherited a small sum; from whom I don't know. Oh, Michael Morey wanted that money. Why should a boy have more than him? Should not the eldest be the one who held the purse strings?

'Come and help your old grandfather at his work,' said Michael Morey, who, being in his sixties, was not as old as all that.

Down to the woods they went, and there Michael Morey hacked off his grandson's head with a bill hook. Then he

hacked off the boy's arms and legs, stuffed them into some old leather saddlebags, and hid them in the undergrowth.

Michael Morey may have been a greedy man, but he wasn't a clever man, so he was soon caught and taken to Winchester to stand trial. He was found guilty and hanged. The body was returned to the Island and a gibbet was erected on an old tumulus, and there the tarred corpse swung in the wind – before it fell to earth and the remains were buried in the old mound.

Should you go to that mound at midnight, and should you circle it widdershins (anticlockwise) twelve times, and then call out 'Michael Morey' three times, his ghost will appear. Why anyone would want to do that is beyond me, but some impressionable ghost hunters recently did so. No one knows what they saw, because none of them will talk about it, but I gather they've all given up ghost hunting. The gibbet post is said to have been incorporated into a beam in the nearby Hare & Hounds pub, and the pub is also said to own the skull of Michael Morey.

It is not a pleasant story, and maybe it has survived as folk-lore because of the unnaturalness of a grandfather murdering his grandson. It could be, though, that the location has kept the story alive, for Michael Morey's Hump is a Bronze Age barrow, which also has Saxon remains buried in it. Should you go there, you will be rewarded by a wonderful view of eastern

Wight. It is one of those singular places, and maybe the grisly tale of Michael Morey has added itself to more ancient stories.

The skull in the Hare & Hounds is much more ancient than Michael Morey; it is from one of the original prehistoric burials.

Tales of Benjamin Snuddon

No one would try and excuse Michael Morey's actions. When we come to smuggling, though – well, it was hardly considered a crime. On the mainland, a lot of smuggling was carried out by organised gangs – some of which, like the Hawkhurst Gang, operated over an area stretching from Kent to Dorset, through Sussex and Hampshire. These were vicious criminals, and murder and torture were part of their stock in trade. On the Isle of Wight, however, smuggling was just a way of life, and there were no big, organised, smuggling gangs, and none of the mainland gangs could get a foothold on the Island. Cork Heads had little time for rule from the mainland anyway. Lots of tales grew up around illicit liquor and the various hiding places for the contraband, and some of them seem to have attached themselves to Benjamin Snuddon, a guileless and innocent man from Niton; or possibly a man who was very full of guile – various stories seem to give contradictory accounts.

Niton is at the very southernmost tip of the Island – next stop France. Of Niton, the nineteenth-century writer Dobell wrote:

The whole population here are smugglers. Everyone has an ostensible occupation, but nobody gets his money by it, or cares to work in it. Here are fishermen who never fish, but always have pockets full of money, and farmers whose farming consists in ploughing the deep by night, and whose daily time is spent standing like herons on lookout posts.

We have to presume that Benjamin Snuddon was an innocent who somehow knew nothing of all this. One night, he was passing through the churchyard with a belly full of beer, and he was unaware that one of the tombs was a hiding place for smuggled goods. As he passed by, a marble slab slowly lifted itself up, and a face appeared.

'What o'clock is it, Benjamin Snuddon?' said the face.

''tis the Day of Judgement,' cried Benjamin, and fled the scene in terror.

Benjamin was prone to misadventures in graveyards. On another occasion, he left the hostelry on a dismal, rainy night. As he stumbled across the churchyard, he failed to notice a freshly dug grave, ready to receive a nice new corpse the next morning. Benjamin tumbled into the waiting hole, and then tried to clamber out. The rain poured down and the more he scrabbled at the wet earth with his fingers, the more he fell back into the waiting grave. Then one of Benjamin's cronies also came staggering out of the pub, across the graveyard, and tumbled into the grave.

'You'll never get out of here, Albert,' said Benjamin, laying his cold, wet, clammy hand on Albert's shoulder.

But, by Christ, Albert did!

Other stories present Benjamin as not only being guileful, rather than guileless, but of being capable of outsmarting both smugglers and excise officers. One day, Benjamin stumbled across a keg of spirits that had been tucked away by the smugglers. He poured the spirits into a milk pail, and then filled the keg with seawater. Tying it about with fishing floats, Benjamin floated the keg out to sea. Off he then went to the coastguard and claimed the reward for discovering contraband. Benjamin reckoned those cows gave the very best milk!

The stories arise, though, from widespread sympathy – indeed involvement – with the smugglers. On the north coast, in Whippingham churchyard, there is an epitaph on a gravestone for a smuggler killed by the excise men, and it reads:

All you that pass pray look and see
How soon my life was took from me
By those officers as you hear
They spilt my blood that was so dear
But God is good, is just and true
And will reward to each their due

Smuggling still takes place around the Island, but now it *is* those criminal gangs. In 2002, smugglers intended to land a £90 million consignment of cocaine at a bay near Ventnor. The weather beat the yacht back to Windy Bay, a mile away, and they had to lug their cargo, like eighteenth-century smugglers, along cliff-top paths. They got nicked.

THE QUEEN OF CHANTILLY

St Helens is on the eastern end of the Island, and is a beautiful place – all set around village greens, with its ruined old church and the sound of the sea. In the 1790s, a smuggler and fisherman called Dicky Daws lived in St Helens, and the family lived well enough – though more on the proceeds of smuggling than the proceeds of fishing. Unfortunately for the family, Dicky Daws was a bit too partial to the liquor that he was smuggling, and the drink killed him. His wife, son and two daughters were left eking out a living winkle picking on Bembridge Beach. They ended up in the workhouse.

When she was thirteen, the youngest daughter, Sophie, went to work on a farm, but as she grew older she realised that her beauty was an asset that could be used; a quality that could lift her out of poverty. The Island couldn't hold her, and she ran away to Portsmouth. She used her sexuality, her cunning, her intelligence, and her capacity for survival, to become an actress in London's Covent Garden, and then become the mistress of a wealthy gentleman from Turnham Green. After this, she was to be found in a brothel in Piccadilly; but this wasn't some seething brothel above an inn, this was a high-class establishment, and she managed to become mistress of the Duc de Bourbon, an exile from revolutionary France. She proved that she had intelligence as well as cunning by successfully receiving an education in French, Latin, Greek and music.

When the Duc de Bourbon returned to France after the fall of Napoleon, Sophie came with him as his daughter, and was married off to a major in the royal guard of Louis XVIII. Unbeknownst to her husband, she continued as the mistress of the Duc de Bourbon, only he was now the Prince de

Condé. She then showed her true loyalty – a loyalty to the past and to her background, a loyalty that gainsays the often rather prurient and slightly disdainful accounts of her life. She brought her mother, her sister Charlotte and her brother James across to France, and installed them on the estate.

The story goes on in a similar vein: Sophie's husband discovered her relationship with Condé, and Sophie was ejected from the court, but she used her powerful personality and got a large slice of Condé's estate. She was received back in court by the next king, Charles X.

Condé was eventually found hanging from a window, and Sophie was suspected of organising his murder. He may well have perished whilst indulging in the solitary pleasure of autoerotic asphyxiation – that we'll never know – but the French public blamed that foreign guttersnipe, Sophie, and they turned against her. So, Sophie ended up living very well in England, where she was known as the Queen of Chantilly. Her brother died before her, and his grave is in St Helens churchyard.

There is also, in St Helens, a cottage on the village green that bears a plaque, a plaque which I saw before I knew the story, and which made me curious. The inscription says:

SOPHIE DAWES
MADAME DE FEUCHERES
Daughter of Richard Dawes
Fisherman & Smuggler
known as
THE QUEEN OF CHANTILLY
was born here
about 1792

So an historical story becomes a legend, and a remarkable woman uses whatever means she can to escape the workhouse and rise to the top of French society. Argentina may have Evita, but the Isle of Wight has Sophie Dawes, Queen of Chantilly.

PEACE, LOVE AND LATRINES

In 1970 I was a teenager hitchhiking south through England, after a visit to Ireland. As I stood by the roadside, I encountered lines of weary, bedraggled, but generally happy people, hitch-hiking north. They were returning home after attending the Isle of Wight Festival. That year there had been 600,000 people attending the festival – more than there had been at Woodstock. The following year, the Isle of Wight Act was passed, preventing gatherings of more than 5,000 people on the Island without a special licence.

But is this folklore? Well, it was such an event – the time when visitors to the Island outnumbered residents, when Jimi Hendrix made his last appearance, the time when the Island was seen by many through a haze of hallucinogenic drugs – that it became so. It became the focus of stories, some exaggerated, and it changed the nature of the Island.

When Queen Victoria had Osborne House built on the Island and spent a lot of time in residence, she opened the Island up to tourism. A lot of well-heeled 'overners' went to live there,

and the Island became famous for the yachting fraternity. It did, however, become a little dull. A lot of those 1970 visitors stayed, or liked the Island and returned. They brought a fresh vigour and, arguably, a greater connection with the old, established Islanders, the Cork Heads. Sometimes, when I wander the Island now, I come across people whose residence started just after 1970, and we can sit and talk about old times and talk about the Island; they seem to have a great love for the place they chose as home. Their children, as with the children of Cork Heads, tend to grow up and leave the Island. As they get older, though, and have children of their own, they often return.

POSTSCRIPT

Guidebooks to Hampshire don't tend to mention the Rowner Estate. This is a housing estate in Gosport, originally built for the Ministry of Defence. If you go past it, though, you come to the Alver Valley Country Park, built on a land-fill site, and a beautiful wooded area. Follow a track down through the woods, and you might smell wood smoke and hear voices. Then you suddenly see a seventeenth-century village: Little Woodham. I enjoy the strange juxtaposition, the fact that you pass through a modern housing estate to get to the village.

Now, I'm a storyteller. I don't need to adopt a persona, or wear funny clothes – I am who I am. As I've said in the introduction, a storyteller can be a man in a hi-viz jacket, sit-ting by a burger van, or a teaching assistant in a school who loves her locality. I am not a re-enactor. Once a year, how-ever, on May Day, I do dress up. I don seventeenth-century clothes and go to Little Woodham. The more serious re-enactors each have a character, and that character has a role; a skill or craft, a place in things. I thought I'd better have a role for my once-a-year visit, and so my character was a tinker and storyteller. The year is 1642, just before the outbreak of civil war, and for fun I wrote, in cod seventeenth-century parlance, the storyteller's story. Here it is. (A hagstone, by the way, is a holed stone; they used to be hung up in Hampshire barns to ensure good luck.)

The Storyteller's Story

I love this land and oft times I do hate it, travelling far distances; from the wild heathes of Dorsetshire to that pox-ridden wen, Portesmouth, where the people have all gone to the Devile and the young men do wear hoodes and do swagger through the streets, and the maidens – who are not maidens – do disport themselves in a lewd and lascivious manner and do show their flesh, though they be distorted by the foul and malodorous food they do eat; for oft times they do eat food from that rascally Scottische victualler MacDonald, who does sell the most vile and noisome con-coctions that do contain the very sweepings of the gutter. And they do destroy the very streets with their bynge drink-ing and they do call themselves chavies.

I do sell many things in many villages: pots and kerchiefs and sweet toys. I do also sell hagestones for to bring good luck to good wifes, though they do sometimes chase me away with their besoms.

More than all I do like to tell stories – and if thou lookest through the eye of a hagestone there be always a story to be told. For I have seen the giant Onion curse, and hurl a boulder at the giant Ascupart; I have seen Ocknell Pond turn red with the blood of a king; I have seen the dancing stones of Titchfield; I have seen the moon hurl madness at the cyder-soaked loo-nies of Tadley; I have seen wonders. These stories are here in Hamptonshire.

But now there are many who will make these stories sinful – who will silence me and call me jabbering heathen – even those who will destroy the miz-mazes of old England and who say that old Shakespeare was a mere prattler. These men will hold all a sin, except for the sin of avarice, and they will cast me forth from the lands they grasp unto themselves with an oath and a boot up the fundament. Shall I meet one on a forest path though, and me with a stout blackthorne or my tinker's knife, then they do sing another song – and they do sing out of their fundament and the boot is on the other foot. And so it is, for why leave a pair of good boots on a dead man?

And yet those who do make sin out of old stories do be telling us wondrous stories from the Bible. Twas I thought the Bible was Latin just for priests and bishops, but there are those who will read the Bible to common folk and those stories of far away and long ago are stories of here and now; folk do talk of Jericho as they would talk of a town that is here; and they do talk of Sodom and Gomorrah as they do talk of Portesmouth and Gosport; and they do tell stories of David and Goliath, and Cain and Abel, and Sampson and Delilah, and an angry God and a gentle son; and these stories are wondrous. And folk do say that the Devile is loose in the land and so I think he may be, though not in the miz-maze, or the nine man's morris, or the song of a maiden.

I have been told of the Phooka, who had the head of a goat and the body of a man and I know he is here in Hamptonshire for I have walked many a Pook's Hill or a Puck's Lane and I have seen his red eyes in the darkness. And they call him Satan and I think he skips across this land – hippetty hoppetty – firing lightning from his eyes and thunderbolts from his arse and he do put madness in the minds of men. For folk do dispute, and brother do turn against brother; and if all the land do fall to hatred and strife, who will buy my wares, and who will listen to my stories?

But I love much. Though life do boot me in the fundament and do rattle my pate with a cudgel; yet I am one of the Lords of No Man's Land, and sometimes I do lie by the fire like Old Lob-lie-by-the-Fire; and sometimes I do lie by the ragged robin in the hedge like Ragged Robin Hood; and oft times I do smell the dew on the grass and feel the sun come through the trees to warm me when I am wet and cold; and sometimes I do walk towards a village and smell the wood smoke and hear the song of a maiden. And these things are pleasures and I am a king. Though now the wenches roll not in my arms but call me sillie old bugger – yet they do at times give me a mug of ale, and the wifes do buy my wares, and the children do listen to my stories, and sometimes the older folk too.

And should I die at Little Woodham I think they will bury me right, and say holy words, and I could want no more than that. But if the Devile has his way and the land comes unto strife, there will be more to bury than I, and holy words will be mere prating.

This was a bit of fun, but it helps remind us that stories are not just about reading books, or looking at websites. They are more about walking the land and exploring your home county, whether that county is your home by adoption or birth. If you are a visitor, that exploration helps you value place and locality, whilst at the same time many of the stories demonstrate a universality. If we explore more, and leave ourselves open to stories, we might be less ready to accept the despoliation of our surroundings, and add pleasure and value to our own lives.

BIBLIOGRAPHY

Books:

Boase, Wendy, *The Folklore of Hampshire and the Isle of Wight* (B.T. Batsford Ltd, London, 1976)

Elder, Abraham, *Tales and Legends of the Isle of Wight: With the Adventures of the Author in Search of Them* (Simpkin, Marshall & Co., London, 1839)

Englefield, Sir Henry, *A Walk through Southampton* (Baker and Fletcher, Piccadilly, 1805)

Hoare, Philip, *England's Lost Eden* (Harper Perennial, London, 2005)

Newman, Chris, *Saints… The Glory Games* (Southampton Reference Library, 2005)

Purslow, Frank (ed.), *Marrow Bones; English Folk Songs from the Hammond and Gardiner MSS* (EFDS publication, 1965)

Sillence, C.M., *Tales of Old West End* (West End Community Association, 1995)

Vesey-Fitzgerald, Brian, *Hampshire and the Isle of Wight* (Robert Hale Ltd, London, 1949)

Wayland's Guide: Isle of Wight, Portsmouth and Dockyard (Wayland, approx. 1885)

Websites:

Alver Valley Country Park, Gosport:
http://www.groundwork-solent.org.uk/land#Alver_Valley_
  Country_Park

Blackwater Valley Countryside Area:
http://www.blackwater-valley.org.uk/valley_history.htm

Bursledon Brickworks:
http://www.bursledonbrickworks.org.uk/

Isle of Wight Stories:
http://www.iwbeacon.com/island-stories.aspxhttp://www.
  iwbeacon.com/island-stories.aspx

The Wilfrid Pilgrimage Trail. Also produced as a booklet, available in Meon Valley churches:
http://www.wilfrid-meon-pilgrimage.co.uk/

Little Woodham, seventeenth-century village, Gosport:
http://www.littlewoodham.org.uk

The author:
http://www.michaelolearystoryteller.com/